Wish You Were Here

Wish You Were Here

Emily's Guide to the 50 States

Kathleen Krull
illustrated by Amy Schwartz

A Doubleday Book for Young Readers

With thanks to Jane Feder; Dorothy A. Coe, Touring Counselor, Automobile
Club of Southern California; the San Diego Public Library; the travel information bureaus of each state; my parents for taking us to states beginning with "M"; Paul Brewer; Nina Kamberos; Mary Horschke for Hawaii;
Donna Keefe, L.Ac.; Pat Laughlin and Robert Burnham; Wendy Barish; and
especially my editor, Mary Cash

—K.K.

I'd like to thank my husband, Leonard, for his assistance with research
and for his loving support.

—A.S.

A Doubleday Book for Young Readers
Published by Bantam Doubleday Dell Publishing Group, Inc.
1540 Broadway
New York, New York 10036
Doubleday and the portrayal of an anchor with a dolphin are
trademarks of Bantam Doubleday Dell Publishing Group, Inc.
Text copyright © 1997 by Kathleen Krull
Illustrations copyright © 1997 by Amy Schwartz

Library of Congress Cataloging-in-Publication Data
Krull, Kathleen.
    Wish you were here : Emily's guide to the 50
states / by Kathleen Krull ; illustrated by Amy Schwartz.
        p.   cm.
    Summary: As they travel from state to state, Emily and her
grandmother introduce the special features and sights of each
of the fifty states.
    ISBN 0-385-31146-X
    1. United States—Guidebooks—Juvenile literature.
[1. United States—Guides.]   I. Schwartz, Amy, ill.   II. Title.
E158.K78   1997
917.304'929—dc20   93-18511   CIP   AC

Manufactured in the United States of America
June 1997
10 9 8 7 6 5 4 3

To Emily in Illinois—as well as Colin, Caitlin, Rebecca, Kevin, Elliot, and Andrew—from their aunt in California

—K.K.

For Debbie Parker

—A.S.

Contents

To Alaska

Washington

North Dakota

Oregon

Montana

Idaho

South Dakota

Wyoming

Nebraska

Nevada

Utah

Colorado

Kansas

California

Oklahoma

Arizona

New Mexico

Texas

To Hawaii

Alaska

Hawaii

Our Route

Introduction

"I have a little red car," she said to me one day. "And you have more curiosity than twelve cats. Don't you think it's time you and I hit the road and discover the United States?"

"She" is my grandmother. She writes very famous books for children. Sometimes she even writes about me, Emily Emerson. I guess I should be used to Grandma's sensational ideas by now. She's a pretty sensational person.

But get this: Grandma wanted to use the whole summer to travel to each and every one of the 50 states! Now, this was a real Adventure. I'd hardly ever been outside of Manhattan. (That's in New York City, in New York State, just in case you don't live here, too.)

So of course I said yes. And my mom and dad said yes. And my geography teacher said, "Hip hip hooray!"

So, the very day after school got out, Grandma and I set off. It was just the two of us, with plenty of guidebooks and paper and pens. And—most important—Grandma's maps.

Well, I had a GREAT time discovering the United States of America. Except for one problem I wonder if other curious explorers have had. I have to admit that I *missed* my mom and dad.

Then Grandma came up with the very best idea of all: writing letters home, to tell all about each state. Letters to show how much I wished Mom and Dad were with us.

Then, when our trip was over, Grandma and I made a book. We put in parts from my letters home, plus some souvenirs, photos, postcards, facts and figures, funny stories, and even certain parts from our diaries. We included Grandma's maps—for people who want to know how we got around.

Grandma wanted our book to explain exactly how each state is different from the others: each state's "claim to fame." And I wanted to show how much fun we had.

So, this is it—*Wish You Were Here: Emily's Guide to the 50 States*, with help from her grandmother. I hope you like it—and that you'll someday be able to discover the United States of America for yourself, in person.

When you do, send your parents or friends a postcard . . . to say, "Having a GREAT time. Wish you were here!"

Emily

New York

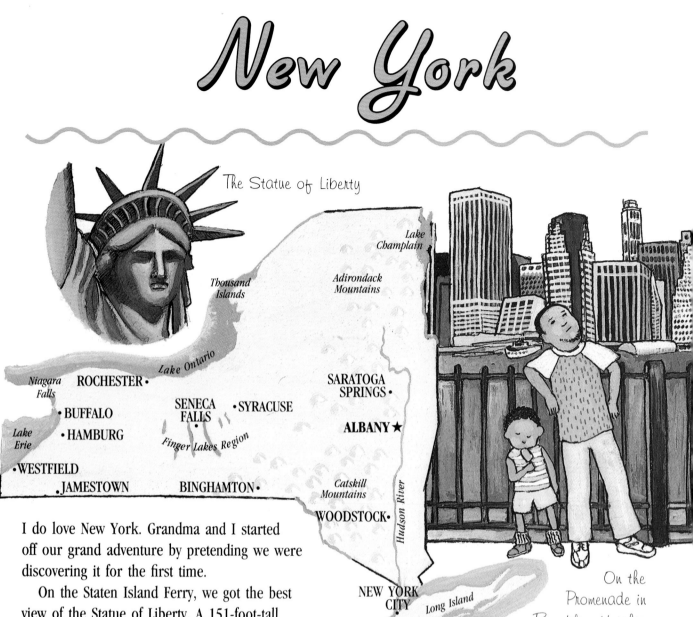

The Statue of Liberty

Lake Champlain

Adirondack Mountains

Thousand Islands

Lake Ontario

Niagara Falls

ROCHESTER •

SARATOGA SPRINGS •

• SYRACUSE

SENECA FALLS

• BUFFALO

ALBANY ★

Lake Erie

• HAMBURG

Finger Lakes Region

• WESTFIELD

Catskill Mountains

• JAMESTOWN

BINGHAMTON •

WOODSTOCK •

Hudson River

NEW YORK CITY

Long Island

On the Promenade in Brooklyn Heights

I do love New York. Grandma and I started off our grand adventure by pretending we were discovering it for the first time.

On the Staten Island Ferry, we got the best view of the Statue of Liberty. A 151-foot-tall woman representing freedom and hope, this was the first thing new immigrants saw. Many people have ancestors who checked in at Ellis Island (right next door to the statue) before entering America.

About four out of ten people in New York State live in New York City—the Big Apple, the largest city in America. We have more *pigeons* than some states have *people*. And those people (not pigeons) speak more than 75 different languages.

Manhattan is the world's most valuable island, $12\frac{1}{2}$ miles long and only $2\frac{1}{2}$ miles wide. We rented bikes and rode around Central Park, a little green forest right in the middle of all the skyscrapers. The most famous skyscraper is the

Empire State Building—the one King Kong climbed on in the old movie. We stopped to hear free concerts from street musicians.

A lot of New York City is *under*ground. Try 722 miles of rumbling subways that carry millions of people around each week.

Some of my favorite Manhattan places are: Greenwich Village (for people-watching); Wall Street (where fortunes are made and lost in a day); Macy's (the world's largest department store); the Metropolitan Museum of Art (the biggest of the dozens of art museums here); Rockefeller Center (famous for its ice-skating rink);

CAPITAL: **Albany**

MOTTO: *Excelsior* (Ever Upward)

Times Square and Broadway (teeming with theaters); the Apollo Theatre in Harlem (where Michael Jackson and many other stars started their careers); and the Plaza Hotel (where the lucky girl in the Eloise books lived). For eating, I like bagels and cream cheese, hot dogs and pretzels from street vendors, and New York pizza (the *best*).

The other boroughs of New York City are: Brooklyn (Grandma loves *A Tree Grows in Brook-lyn* by Betty Smith, and I love *Where the Wild Things Are* by Brooklyn-born Maurice Sendak); Queens (home to Rockaway Beach, where the largest waves are); Staten Island (where someone invented the first gumball machines); and the Bronx (home to Yankee Stadium).

But guess what: New York is more than just New York City.

In the far north are the Thousand Islands (actually 1,800) and the Adirondack Mountains. Nearby Syracuse gets more snow than any other American city. Honeymooners like Niagara Falls, the spectacular thundering waterfall near Buffalo. And Buffalo is where the song "Buffalo Gals" began.

In the Hudson River valley are towns that inspired Washington Irving to write his headless horseman story, "The Legend of Sleepy Hollow." Nearby Woodstock became famous for a rock music festival in 1969. And the first women's rights convention took place in Seneca Falls.

Westfield is known for grape juice, Saratoga Springs for potato chips and springwater.

And any state that has a *ladybug* as its state insect is my kind of place.

Niagara Falls

3

Pennsylvania

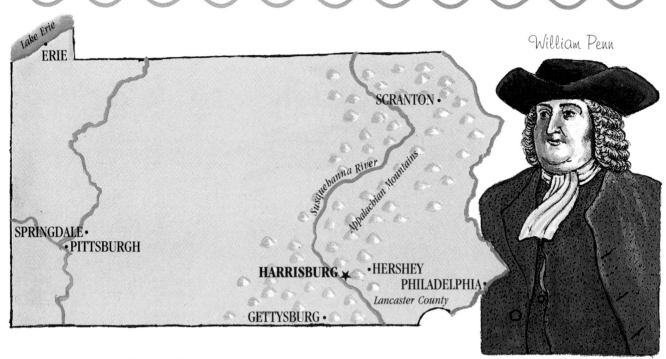

William Penn

Independence Hall

Pennsylvania is the world's mushroom capital, the place where crayons come from, and the state where I learned why the Fourth of July is so important.

A redbrick building on Chestnut Street in Philadelphia, now known as Independence Hall, was the place to be on July 4, 1776. That's the day people from the 13 colonies signed the Declaration of Independence there. It was the birth of the United States of America.

Grandma and I walked all around Independence National Historical Park. I can see why it's called the most historic square mile in America. We saw the Betsy Ross House, where it's said that America's first flag was stitched. The Liberty Bell, which rang out on that first Fourth of July, is most famous of all. But get this—it has a crack in it!

Like real Philadelphians, we put mustard on our soft pretzels. This is a food place. Try Phila-

delphia cream cheese or a submarine sandwich. Root beer showed up here first—and also bananas, seen as very weird at the time.

"It certainly has a great quantity of smoke hanging over it"—that's what the writer Charles Dickens once said of Pittsburgh. Grandma told me the city's motto used to be: "A smoky Pittsburgh is a healthy Pittsburgh." In the old days, this was a manufacturing town, where streetlights had to be turned on at noon and children worked long days in factories. But Grandma and I liked Pittsburgh. It's so much cleaner these days! And the children get to play. Many people think this is now one of America's best places to live.

How do you get away from the rushing big cities? We visited Lancaster County, where the Pennsylvania Dutch (their ancestors actually came from Germany) decorate their barns with signs called roundels. A special group of Pennsylvania Dutch are the Amish, or Plain People, who keep their old-fashioned way of life. They wear plain black clothes, drive horse-drawn buggies, *and have no TV.* We watched girls sewing bonnets and hand-dipping candles, and Grandma bought a soft Amish quilt as a souvenir.

Grandma meeting you-know-who during Gettysburg Civil War Heritage Days

Nearby Gettysburg inspired possibly the most famous speech of all time—you know, "Fourscore and seven years ago. . . ." Abraham Lincoln wrote the Gettysburg Address to dedicate a cemetery here, site of a Civil War battle.

An Amish quilt

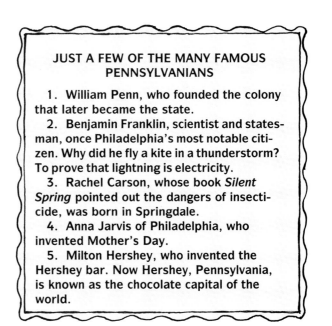

JUST A FEW OF THE MANY FAMOUS PENNSYLVANIANS

1. William Penn, who founded the colony that later became the state.

2. Benjamin Franklin, scientist and statesman, once Philadelphia's most notable citizen. Why did he fly a kite in a thunderstorm? To prove that lightning is electricity.

3. Rachel Carson, whose book *Silent Spring* pointed out the dangers of insecticide, was born in Springdale.

4. Anna Jarvis of Philadelphia, who invented Mother's Day.

5. Milton Hershey, who invented the Hershey bar. Now Hershey, Pennsylvania, is known as the chocolate capital of the world.

5

Ohio

Cincinnati is a place where pigs fly.

Well, just in one spot, actually—the Ohio River front, where statues of winged pigs celebrate the city's history as a pork capital. It was known as Porkopolis! Writer Charles Dickens once called Cincinnati "a beautiful city, cheerful, thriving, animated." I wonder if, when he visited, he danced the polka and ate and ate the way Grandma and I did: stuffed cabbage, Hungarian hot dogs, and pierogi, the Polish version of ravioli.

Ohio might look mostly like one giant farm, with ordinary corn and sleepy sheep. But Ohioans know how to have a party. They have more festivals than any other state. The State Fair in Columbus—with carnival rides, farm exhibits, and contests—is the largest annual fair in the world. Cincinnati's Kidsfest is said to be America's largest one-day event devoted to children. The Pumpkin Show in Circleville has pumpkin-burgers, while the Twins Day Festival in Twinsburg has twins who come from around the world. Two of the ten most popular theme parks in America are in Ohio—Cedar Point Park in Sandusky (said to have the fastest roller coaster in the world) and Kings Island in Cincinnati.

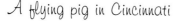

A flying pig in Cincinnati

Cedar Point amusement park in Sandusky

CAPITAL: **Columbus**

MOTTO: **With God, All Things Are Possible**

Rural Ohio

Ohio loves sports. The Cincinnati Reds were the first professional baseball team, back in 1869. At the Pro Football Hall of Fame in Canton, we craned our necks to look at a seven-foot statue of Jim Thorpe, the first really big football star. We also saw the entire history of professional football, in video and exhibits.

Ohio also loves music. The term "rock and roll" was invented in Cleveland, which happens to be home to the Rock and Roll Hall of Fame.

Cleveland's "emerald necklace" of pretty parks circles the city. The parks must be good for reading—the library system here is more heavily used than almost any other in America. (Two other Ohio cities, Dayton and Toledo, are in the top five for most library books loaned per person.)

Columbus likes to be in the middle of things. "The largest small town in America" is in the exact center of Ohio, with the town square at *its* very center. Lots of companies use Columbus as a test market for new products.

Presidents love Ohio—*seven* of them were born here: Ulysses S. Grant, Rutherford B. Hayes, James A. Garfield, Benjamin Harrison, William McKinley, William Howard Taft, and Warren G. Harding. Lois Lenski, author of many children's books, was born here, as was Annie Oakley, the American markswoman. William McGuffey began teaching in Ohio and is the author of the first children's textbooks (they were called McGuffey's Readers). Rod Serling, who created *The Twilight Zone* on TV, went to school here.

The most famous words spoken by an Ohioan? Probably "One small step for a man, one giant leap for mankind"—said by astronaut Neil Armstrong as he was setting foot on the moon in 1969. John Glenn, the first astronaut to orbit the earth, also started out as a baby from Ohio.

But for my *favorite* Ohioan, I'd probably pick Clarence Crane. He invented Life Savers right here, in Cleveland, Ohio.

Transporting steel mill supplies in Cleveland

Kentucky

What do horses and music have in common?

It's a grass that really *is* blue—in the Bluegrass state of Kentucky.

In the middle of Kentucky, the world's horse capital, are thousands of square miles of rolling land. Thousands of handsome horses munch on blue meadows divided by miles of white fences. The most famous horse race ever takes place every May at Churchill Downs in Louisville. It's the Kentucky Derby, and people call it "the most exciting two minutes in sports." At Kentucky Horse Park in Lexington, I went for a pony ride—and I *didn't* fall off!

Bluegrass *music* started in Kentucky. We kept the sounds of fiddle, mandolin, and banjo on our car radio while we visited Appalachia, where many of my favorite folk songs come from. The people here are poor, but their culture is rich—stories, songs, and dances brought from the British Isles.

For a state song, "My Old Kentucky Home" is pretty famous. Stephen Foster wrote it about a real home that still stands. Old Talbott Tavern, a nearby restaurant, is where Daniel Boone, Abraham Lincoln, and outlaw Jesse James all ate their meals, but probably not at the same time.

We stopped for Shaker lemon pie at Shakertown at Pleasant Hill. Grandma told me all about the Shakers, an interesting religious group founded by Ann Lee. They invented things like clothespins, washing machines, seed packets, and apple parers. We watched people making quilts, baskets, candles, and furniture. I bought handmade soap as a souvenir.

We went underground for lunch . . . to Mammoth Cave, the biggest cave system in the world. Try 330 miles of passages cut into the earth by the Green River. It's a whole world down here: waterfalls, rooms high enough to hold a 12-story building, and unusual animals—like eyeless fish, white spiders, and bats the size of my thumbnails.

After that, we were happy to see blue sky

My favorite Kentuckians!

CAPITAL: **Frankfort**

MOTTO: **United We Stand, Divided We Fall**

again. We visited Cumberland Gap National Histori-
cal Park, where Daniel Boone helped build the
Wilderness Road across the mountains. Much of
Kentucky looks the same now as when it was the
newest "frontier," the first state west of the misty
Appalachian Mountains.

We picnicked in Daniel Boone National Forest,
at the Yahoo Falls Scenic Area. In 1810, Princess
Cornblossom, the leader of a Cherokee tribe,
gathered her people here and prepared to leave
Kentucky. But before they could leave, they were
massacred by settlers.

On clear nights, when there's a full moon at
Cumberland Falls State Resort Park, you can see
a moonbow: a nighttime rainbow. And near here
is the Kentucky restaurant where Colonel Harland
Sanders developed his secret recipe for fried
chicken. Hmm, now I know why it isn't called,
say, Massachusetts Fried Chicken!

**THINGS TO WATCH OUT FOR IN
KENTUCKY**

Kentucky state law says that every person must take a bath once a year. And in
Lexington, it's illegal to carry an ice-cream
cone in your pocket.

Boonesboro, founded by Daniel Boone, 1775

Mammoth Cave

Ohio River

★ FRANKFORT
LOUISVILLE
• LEXINGTON
• BOONESBORO

Daniel Boone
National Forest

Green River

Mammoth Cave

Cumberland Falls
State Resort Park

Cumberland Gap
National Historical
Park

Appalachian Mountains

Indiana

On our way to the Indiana Dunes State Park, we saw smokestacks—a sign of heavy industry. But the dunes are all-natural —great piles of golden sand. Indiana knows how to make the most of its 45 miles of Lake Michigan shoreline.

We picked our own strawberries at a place by the road—and ate them. Many people think Indiana is typical America: flat and farmy scenes dotted with small villages. But smack in the middle of everything is the big city of Indianapolis.

Most people probably don't know that here in Indianapolis, Gilbert Van Camp invented canned pork and beans just before the Civil War. But everyone's heard of the Indianapolis 500. Indianapolis—before Detroit, Michigan, took over as the Motor City—was home to 45 car manufacturers. Now it honors that past with the Indy 500. Every Memorial Day, a third of a million people come and cheer for cars in the most exciting race in America.

Vroom!

The *Little* 500 is a 50-mile bicycle race in the rolling hills of Bloomington. Indiana is a good state for bicycles: It has 800 miles of roads marked as the Hoosier Bikeway System.

Biking on the Hoosier Bikeway System

CAPITAL: **Indianapolis**
MOTTO: **Crossroads of America**

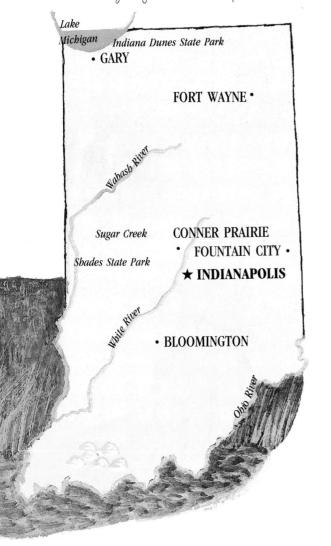

Shooting a few in Indianapolis

Lake Michigan
Indiana Dunes State Park
• GARY

FORT WAYNE •

Wabash River

Sugar Creek   CONNER PRAIRIE
• FOUNTAIN CITY •
Shades State Park
★ **INDIANAPOLIS**

White River

• BLOOMINGTON

Ohio River

We visited the Children's Museum in Indianapolis, the largest children's museum in the world, with PLEASE TOUCH signs everywhere. In a playground nearby, we saw a fast game of basketball. Hoosiers are wild about hoops.

To the west, Shades State Park has ridges 100 feet tall, carved out by streams. All that shade made things sort of gloomy. Early settlers called this area Shades of Death and had stories about possible murders here. We took a canoe ride down Sugar Creek, through the middle of the park. I pictured what it must have been like when the Shawnee and the Miami, American Indian peoples, used to live in Indiana.

To the east, Conner Prairie is said to be one of the ten best places to relive America's past. It's a whole village re-creating the houses, costumes, and customs of 1836 Indiana. Nearby Fountain City was the Grand Central Station of the Underground Railroad. It wasn't a real railroad, but instead a Civil War–time secret network leading enslaved blacks to Canada or safe places in northern states.

We stopped for elephant ears (the favorite pastry in Indiana) and crullers in Fort Wayne. This was the home of Johnny Appleseed, a real person named John Chapman in the 1800's. He planted thousands of apple trees—the seeds for orchards in the Midwest. He probably saw more of America than any other person of his day. We saluted him by eating apple dumplings, biscuits with apple butter, and apple ice cream.

Crunchy apples

11

Michigan

We try out a Model T

BE 2789

If it wasn't for something practically invented in Michigan . . . Grandma and I wouldn't be taking this trip. Right—the *car*!

Two different Michiganians (R. E. Olds and Henry Ford) had each developed automobiles by 1896. Soon Oldsmobiles were selling for $650, and Ford's Model T, the Tin Lizzie, became one of the most popular cars ever made.

Detroit is the automobile capital of the U.S.A., or the Motor City, or just plain Motown. At nearby Dearborn, we learned lots about cars at the Henry Ford Museum and Greenfield Village. I can see why it's the most visited indoor-outdoor museum in America.

But Michigan is a water wonderland—a better place for *boats* than cars! Try 11,000 inland lakes, thousands of miles of rivers, and four huge Great Lakes. Michigan is the only state bordered by four out of the five. This gives it more fresh water than any other state.

With all that water, Michigan is the only state that comes in two parts. The Upper Peninsula has 150 waterfalls, and more deer, elk, and bear than people. All around are stacks of firewood—the winters must be cold up here!

The Lower Peninsula looks like a mitten (on the map, that is). It has most of the people, the

CAPITAL: **Lansing**

MOTTO: *Si Quaeris Peninsulam Amoenam Circumspice*
(If You Seek a Pleasant Peninsula, Look About You)

Bond Falls on the Ontonagon River

Michigan has more campsites than any other state, and millions of acres of parks, forests, and beaches. It has "tunnels of trees" and more kinds that change color—try 65—than any other state.

My favorite thing about Michigan? The fireflies. I'll never forget the night we caught 'em and put 'em in jars to watch their shiny blinks.

The next morning, we took a ferryboat from Ludington, across Lake Michigan to Wisconsin. We put our car underneath, while we sat on deck and ate something this state is famous for—fudge. Here in Michigan tourists like us are called fudgies.

AMAZING MICHIGAN STORIES

1. French explorers reached Michigan two years before the Pilgrims reached Massachusetts. They thought they were on their way to the Orient.

2. A French trapper named Antoine de la Mothe *Cadillac* founded Detroit! Other famous Michiganians are former President Gerald Ford, the rock singer Madonna, and Ernest Hemingway, who wrote stories about northern Michigan.

3. The only way Michigan was allowed to become a state was to trade part of its border near Ohio for most of the Upper Peninsula.

---

best farmland, and quiet towns with steepled churches. Grand Rapids is said to have more churches per person than any other American city, while Holland has the only authentic Dutch windmill in America and a Tulip Time Festival every May.

We stopped in Battle Creek for a bowl of . . . cereal! Dr. John Kellogg invented granola and corn flakes here, and C. W. Post invented Grape Nuts. Now more breakfast cereal is made in Battle Creek—the cereal bowl of America—than anywhere else in the world.

Taking the ferry across Lake Michigan

Wisconsin

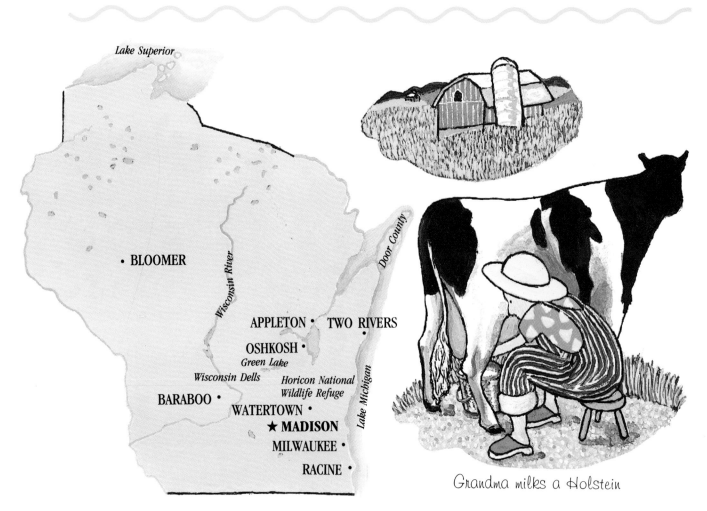

Grandma milks a Holstein

Holy cow!

This state gets my vote for the most cows. At first Grandma and I tried to count them as we drove along. But we had to give up. Well, we're talking almost *two million* Holsteins, Jerseys, Guernseys, and others that produce milk, butter, ice cream, and almost *two billion* pounds of cheese a year. We visited a factory to watch cheese being made. Did you know all cheese starts out white? A vegetable dye is added later to make it yellow or orange. And did you know that Wisconsin makes almost half of all the cheese in America? Well, I think I just explained why Wisconsin license plates say AMERICA'S DAIRYLAND!

In Oshkosh, Grandma and I stopped to buy

OshKosh B'gosh overalls—in different sizes, of course. Then we went fishing in Green Lake, the deepest lake in the state. Too bad—the fish weren't biting. Luckily, it was Friday, which just happens to be fish fry night in restaurants all over Wisconsin.

At the cheese factory

CAPITAL: **Madison**
MOTTO: **Forward**

Bratwurst!

Wisconsin is one of the best places to eat I ever saw. You can eat German bratwurst, Norwegian lutefisk (a flaky fish), Cornish pasties (pies stuffed with meat and vegetables), Swedish meatballs, and Danish *kringle* (a delicious pastry). Oscar Mayer hot dogs are made here. The first malted milk ever was made in Racine, and the first ice-cream sundae ever was made in Two Rivers.

Besides cows, I noticed a lot of vacationers. Much of Wisconsin is public forests—perfect for anything outdoors, especially in the fall, when the trees change colors in a sensational colorama. Water, water everywhere: 15,000 pretty blue lakes for fishing, swimming, and boating, and hundreds of waterfalls for picture taking. Water even in the winter: Wisconsin has 1,600 snowplows, which tells you something about how many blizzards it has!

EIGHT WISCONSIN HOT SPOTS

1. Milwaukee, the largest city, an important seaport on Lake Michigan, home to an outstanding zoo and 2,600 bowling alleys.
2. Horicon National Wildlife Refuge stops traffic twice a year when hundreds of thousands of Canada geese use it as a rest stop.
3. Wisconsin Dells, where the Wisconsin River has cut weird formations into the soft sandstone rocks.
4. Door County, famous for fish boils, arts and crafts, and more miles of shoreline than any other county in America.
5. Baraboo, where the Ringling Brothers started off. The Circus World Museum has daily shows and a huge collection of circus equipment.
6. Watertown, where the first U.S. kindergarten was started in 1856.
7. Bloomer, the jump rope capital of the world.
8. Appleton, where people hold séances every Halloween to try to bring back the spirit of Harry Houdini. One of the greatest magicians who ever lived, he was from Appleton, and he died *on* Halloween. Holy cow!

The Wisconsin Dells

15

Illinois

Grandma and I were a quarter of a mile up in the air. From the top of the Sears Tower, we looked down over 29 miles of Lake Michigan shoreline and the bright lights and big city of Chicago. This building, the tallest in the world, has almost as many elevators (104) as it has stories (110). On windy days, and Chicago *is* known as the Windy City, the top of the building can sway six inches.

I found out that Chicago began as a trading post established by Jean Baptiste Point du Sable, a successful black fur trader. Then, in 1871, Mrs. O'Leary's cow knocked over a kerosene lantern and started a fire that destroyed almost the entire city.

Chicago is now the biggest city in the Midwest. Chances are good that any food, person (like a grandmother!), or supply going across the country passes through here. O'Hare is the busiest airport in the world, and Chicago is the busiest railway hub and one of the busiest ports.

Downtown is called the Loop, after the elevated train (the "El") tracks that make a circle around it. Grandma liked the gigantic steel sculpture by Picasso (which is supposed to be a woman's head). I liked a castlelike building called the Water Tower. I bought a box of famous Frango mints at Marshall Field's as a souvenir.

Sears Tower

16 Testing the wind in the Windy City at the Buckingham Memorial Fountain

CAPITAL: **Springfield**

MOTTO: **State Sovereignty—National Union**

At Wrigley (as in the gum) Field, we watched the Chicago Cubs play baseball. We cheered like crazy in between bites of peanuts, popcorn, and something invented in Chicago: Cracker Jack.

Much of the rest of Illinois is prairie and farmland. It's second only to Iowa in hog farming and corn production. Moline is the farm tool capital of America, while Peoria, in the middle of cornfields, is said to represent what Americans think outside the big cities. Now I know what people mean when they say "How will it play in Peoria?"

Presidents like Illinois. Ronald Reagan was born in Tampico and grew up in Dixon. Ulysses S. Grant lived for a time in Galena. Abraham Lincoln worked in Illinois. Near Charleston, we visited the Lincoln Log Cabin State Historical Site. This was where Lincoln lived when he wasn't on the road as a lawyer. Costumed men and women act the parts of Lincoln's neighbors going about their chores.

Illinois has more buildings designed by architect Frank Lloyd Wright than any other state. The world's first Tinkertoys were made in Evanston, and Metropolis is known as Superman's hometown. And Des Plaines is home to the first McDonald's, which looks the same as it did in 1955. Oak Brook is headquarters for its 11,000 restaurants (and 70 billion hamburgers a year).

MOST FAMOUS CHICAGO QUOTE

"Hog butcher for the world,
Tool maker, stacker of wheat,
Player with railroads and the nation's
   freight handler;
Stormy, husky, brawling,
City of the big shoulders."
   —Carl Sandburg (born in Galesburg)

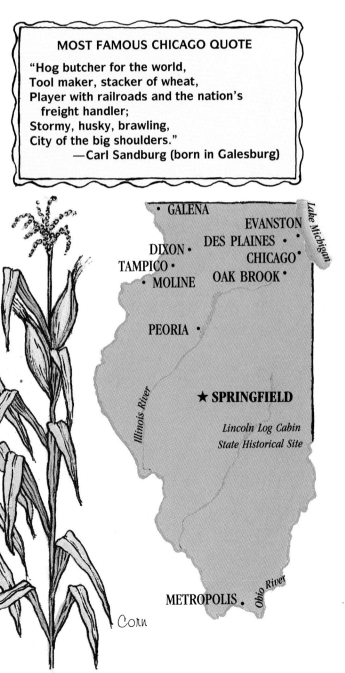

Lincoln's parents' log cabin in Lerna

Corn

GALENA
EVANSTON
DES PLAINES
DIXON
CHICAGO
TAMPICO
OAK BROOK
MOLINE
Lake Michigan

PEORIA

Illinois River

★ SPRINGFIELD

Lincoln Log Cabin
State Historical Site

METROPOLIS
Ohio River

17

Iowa

Feeding the pigs
in Iowa

As we munched our way through ears of juicy sweet corn, we cheered for corny Iowa. This state is first in popcorn—the world's largest popcorn-processing plant is in Sioux City. Most years it is also first in corn production. The tallest cornstalk in the world once grew in Washington, Iowa—31 feet!

Grandma and I put on a pair of bib overalls (28 percent of all Iowans own a pair) and visited one of Iowa's many farms. We collected eggs from the chickens, fed the pigs, and helped to milk a cow. Wow! I hated pulling weeds, but I liked petting the sheep and riding around on a tractor. Grandma loved baking bread, churning butter, and gathering berries. We were ready for big meals: fresh eggs, garden vegetables, and at least five kinds of pies. Whew—farming is very hard work. Grandma said that most farmers work 11 hours a day.

It's easy to see why the Iowa State Fair, in Des Moines in August, is such a big deal. It has 100 carnival rides, Iowa's largest art show, and activities celebrating fruits, vegetables, and livestock.

Iowa is smack between the Missouri and Mississippi Rivers. When we drove around, it looked

Pies at the state fair!

like flat carpets of corn, grain, hay. Because Iowa is right in the middle of America, many people think it represents "middle opinions," too. Iowans get to support a candidate for president first—in open party caucuses held before any presidential primary. Politicians have to pay attention to what Iowans think—or else they're weeded out before the rest of America has any say.

Iowa is the place to see marching bands. We

CAPITAL: **Des Moines**

MOTTO: **Our Liberties We Prize and Our Rights We Will Maintain**

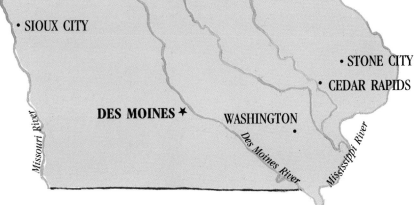

The Mason City marching band

heard the best band concert in Mason City. Meredith Willson wrote *The Music Man,* a whole musical about marching bands, modeling his town on this one. Meanwhile, Czech composer Antonín Dvořák wrote his famous *New World* symphony on a visit to Spillville. Near Cedar Rapids is Stone City, where the artist Grant Wood started an art school. His paintings of rural Iowa include the famous "American Gothic."

"Go West, young man, go West!" is what newspaperman Horace Greeley said to Josiah Grinnell, who moved to Iowa and named a town after himself there. Grandma and I think Greeley meant women, too, and we were glad we went West to Iowa.

From Grandma's Diary

Iowa is great for books. No other state has so many of its people able to read and write, or checks out more library books per person.

Farmy Iowa

A FEW WORDS ABOUT DIRT

1. Very black soil is one reason why Iowa is the heart of America's Corn Belt. The other reasons are an average summer temperature of 70 degrees, frequent showers, and a growing season of at least 140 days.

2. Iowa has less than two percent of the land in America, but one-fourth the Grade A topsoil. No wonder it's said that "Iowa feeds the nation."

3. "It looks good enough to eat."
   —what Robert Frost said about Iowa soil

Minnesota

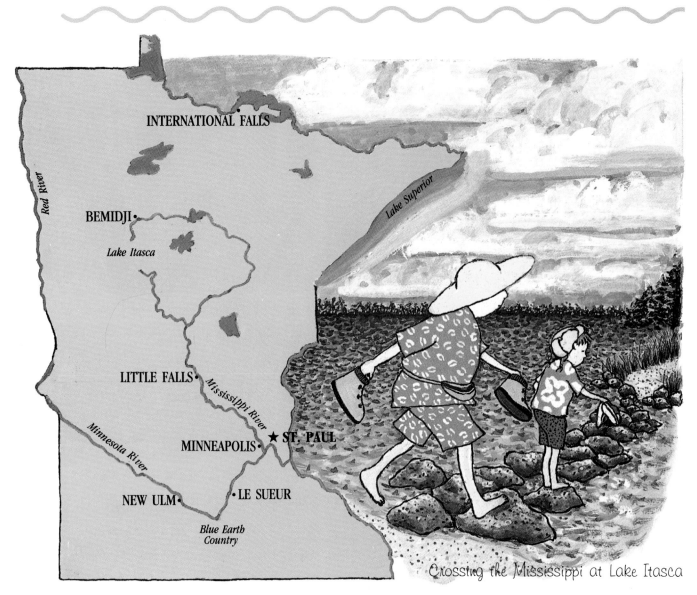

Crossing the Mississippi at Lake Itasca

Minnesota license plates say LAND OF 10,000 LAKES. But it's a lie. There are even *more*—try over 15,000.

We visited just one—Lake Itasca, at Itasca State Park. We took off our shoes and took five shivery steps right across the Mississippi River. Here is where it begins, a baby compared to the "Old Man River" it becomes as it flows 2,340 miles to New Orleans and the Gulf of Mexico.

Grandma says that, according to evidence from buffalo bones here, people have lived near this

water for 4,000 years! Inside the dense woods are some of the largest and oldest red Norway pine trees around. Also bears, deer, wolves, moose, blue herons, and bald eagles.

Minnesota summers are long, but Minnesota winters are longer. In some places, indoor sky-walks protect Minnesotans from the blizzards. One town, International Falls, is known as the ice-box of the nation. Brrr! Still, except for Hawaii, people in Minnesota live longer than anywhere else in America. This state is ranked the best for

CAPITAL: **St. Paul**

MOTTO: *L'Etoile du Nord* **(The Star of the North)**

keeping the environment clean. (And people know how to fix things in Minnesota: Scotch tape was invented here.)

Are the *Twin* Cities of Minneapolis and St. Paul brothers, or sisters, or what? For sure, they're not identical twins. They do face each other, on either side of the Mississippi River, and after some cities in Oklahoma, they have the most American Indian residents, mostly Sioux and Ojibwa. But Minneapolis is larger. It's more Scandinavian, especially Swedish and Norwegian. It has Lake Hiawatha, Minnehaha Parkway and Park, and other streets inspired by Henry Wadsworth Longfellow's *The Song of Hiawatha.*

The other twin, St. Paul, is the capital. It's more German and Irish. The writer F. Scott Fitzgerald was from here. Nearby Anoka is the hometown of writer Garrison Keillor. Grandma told me about a town he invented called Lake Wobegon, where "all the children are above average." A little farther away is New Ulm, where Wanda Gag, who wrote *Millions of Cats,* was born.

I like the way it doesn't get dark in the summer till late in Minnesota. This state has the northernmost point of the entire United States (except Alaska), with Canada as its northern border. Grandma and I stayed up late, listening to the spooky sounds of loons, the state birds, calling to each other across this, the "land of sky blue waters."

Paul Bunyan and Babe

SOME VERY BIG MINNESOTANS

1. People in many places—but especially in Bemidji—tell tall tales about Paul Bunyan, the giant lumberjack as strong as a hundred men. We found out how the Mississippi River was formed (Paul Bunyan accidentally tipped over the tub he was washing his clothes in) and why Minnesota has so many lakes (because everywhere Paul Bunyan stepped, a lake formed).

2. In a place called Blue Earth Country, where the valleys are *green,* we saw the Jolly Green Giant Statue. Nearby Le Sueur is famous for peas.

3. In Little Falls is the boyhood home of famous aviator Charles Lindbergh.

An ice sculpture at the St. Paul Winter Carnival

North Dakota

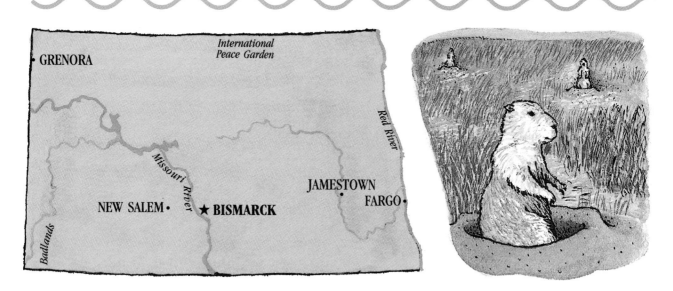

"Why is this land so bad?" I asked Grandma. "Is this where people go who are bad? Or where they go to *be* bad? Or what?"

A buffalo

We were in the beautiful Badlands of North Dakota, and Grandma was laughing. Then she explained how early Sioux settlers called this area "land bad" because it was so rugged and hard to live in.

Truly, the Badlands are a weird landscape—spooky rock formations twisted into different shapes and colors. Some layers are the color of mustard. Volcanic ash caused the blue layers, while lightning bolts set the coal layers on fire, adding bright red and pink. Swift streams cut through everything and created soaring cliffs and sharp spires. Some of those underground coal fires burn all the time, giving off a reddish glow that can be seen for miles.

It's amazing to think of the strange creatures that once lived here: tiny three-toed horses, saber-toothed tigers, ancient camels, dinosaurs like triceratops. I wish I could have seen the largest of all, the titanothere. According to legend the Sioux found its bones and called it Thunderhorse, believing that it came down from the sky during thunderstorms and killed buffalo.

But some buffalo obviously survived, because

CAPITAL: **Bismarck**

MOTTO: **Liberty and Union, Now and Forever, One and Inseparable**

Visiting a dog town

many bees live here, sucking on sweet clover blossoms. Farms here have no mountains or trees to protect against hot summers and cold winters. Fargo-Moorhead, in fact, is said to be the coldest area in America. But people find lots to sing about anyway: The song "Red River Valley" comes from the fertile farming area to the east. We had fun eating German-Russian food, seeing American Indian art and dance, hearing cowboy poetry, and shopping for Scandinavian arts and crafts.

they live in the Badlands now along with pronghorn antelope, bighorn sheep, golden eagles, and coyotes. I liked the prairie dogs. They're not really dogs, but rodents that squeal if you get too close. Their underground colonies are called dog towns.

A good place in North Dakota to think peaceful thoughts is the International Peace Garden. We had a picnic in this park honoring the friendship of America and Canada—the longest border between two peaceful countries in the world. On a monument is carved "As long as men shall live, we will not take up arms against one another." Grandma loved the huge flowery flags of both countries.

Other big things in North Dakota: The world's largest Holstein cow stops traffic in New Salem— the fiberglass cow's name is Salem Sue. The world's largest buffalo is in Jamestown—try three stories tall. The Writing Rock, near Grenora, is a huge boulder covered with prehistoric American Indian pictographs, or picture writing.

North Dakota is first in sunflower seeds, and

HOW TO BECOME PRESIDENT

"If it had not been for what I learned during the years spent in North Dakota, I never would have been president of the United States."

—Theodore Roosevelt

Sunny sunflowers

23

South Dakota

Mount Rushmore

Grandma kept saying that Mount Rushmore was best when seen in morning light. No wonder I was still yawning when I first saw it: the heads of four American presidents—Theodore Roosevelt, George Washington, Abraham Lincoln, and Thomas Jefferson. But there's something about seeing heads that are six stories high that made me wake up fast.

Carved into the side of a stone mountain, Mount Rushmore is said to be the largest human-made sculpture in the world. You could stand up in Washington's eye, for example—although climbing this monument is prohibited. And it's not even finished—it was originally planned to show the four men to their waists. A few miles away, there's another famous unfinished monument: American Indian hero Crazy Horse on his horse, carved out of a mountainside. It's not as far along as Mount Rushmore, but it will be huge. A five-room house will be able to fit inside the horse's nostril.

We were in the famous Black Hills, which I think should be called the Black-Green Hills. South Dakota shares them with Wyoming, and they're covered with the black and green of pine and fir trees. Or maybe they should be called the Gold Hills. This is the place where someone said, "There's gold in them thar hills."

No kidding! South Dakota is first in gold, and the Homestake Gold Mine here, at Lead, produces more gold than just about any other mine—even today. Grandma bought a very small piece of Black Hills gold jewelry as a souvenir.

On Needles Highway

24

CAPITAL: **Pierre**

MOTTO: **Under God the People Rule**

Lead's sister city is Deadwood. In its cemetery are Calamity Jane and her friend Wild Bill Hickok. Calamity Jane (whose real name was Martha Jane Cannary Burk) was a famous frontierswoman and Indian scout and an expert at riding and shooting.

Winding through the Black Hills is Needles Highway, which shows off the "needles," or scary-looking stone spires. The highway is scary, too, taking our car through tunnels we were *sure* we'd never fit through.

Baaaa! South Dakota has twice as many sheep as people. It also has the largest concentration of American Indians, mostly Sioux, of any Great Plains state. A famous creek here called Wounded Knee was the site of clashes between American Indians and whites in the last century and this one, too.

Mitchell is the corn capital of the world, while nearby De Smet is not just any little town on the prairie. Right—it's *the* "Little Town on the Prairie," made famous by Laura Ingalls Wilder. She lived in a log cabin here, and grew up to write all the Little House books about her prairie childhood.

Grandma at the Corn Palace

WHAT DO NORTH AND SOUTH DAKOTA HAVE IN COMMON?

A mystery: To the Sioux people, also known as the Dakotas, "dakota" meant "league of friends." I guess the league was so big it had to split in two. It's easy to think of them as one big Dakota, but Grandma said the Senate wanted more senators. So the Dakota Territory became two states, and it's a big mystery which one became a state first. President Benjamin Harrison deliberately shuffled the papers so no one would ever know.

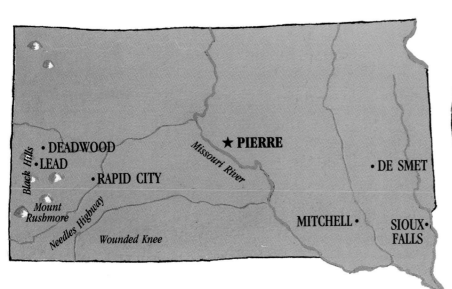

DEADWOOD
LEAD
Black Hills
RAPID CITY
Mount Rushmore
Needles Highway
Wounded Knee
Missouri River
★ PIERRE
DE SMET
MITCHELL
SIOUX FALLS

Laura Ingalls Wilder

Nebraska

Nebraska is a great place to try out your wheels!

"Just how flat is Nebraska?" I asked.

"Flat enough to roller-skate all the way through!" said Grandma.

We were at the National Museum of Roller Skating in Lincoln—the only place in the world devoted to old and new skates, famous skaters, and great moments in skating. Nearby, we rented some skates ourselves and went for a spin in flat Nebraska.

Some people think Nebraska is so flat that it's boring, just waving fields of wheat as far as the eye can see. Back when this was called the Great American Desert, thousands of wagon trains passed through . . . on their way elsewhere. The Czech and German pioneers who did stay couldn't help noticing that something was missing— namely, trees. There was not a lot you could use to build a house with, but pioneer women were smart. They built sod houses, or huts made of

dirt and grass. The fences surrounding these sod houses had old cowboy boots upside down on the fenceposts. To this day, no one knows why. But now Nebraska has the only national forest completely planted by people, and Arbor Day

A pioneer sod house

CAPITAL: **Lincoln**

MOTTO: **Equality Before the Law**

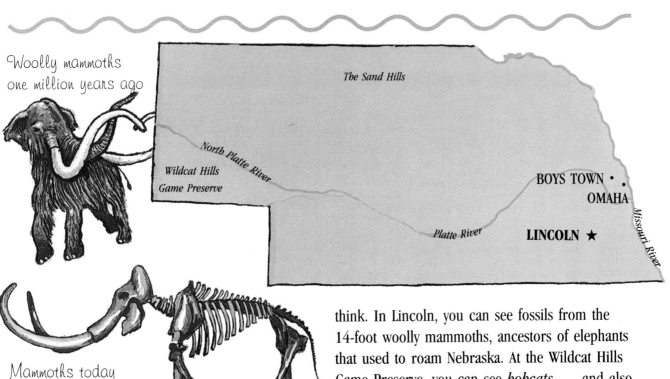

Woolly mammoths one million years ago

Mammoths today

think. In Lincoln, you can see fossils from the 14-foot woolly mammoths, ancestors of elephants that used to roam Nebraska. At the Wildcat Hills Game Preserve, you can see *bobcats* . . . and also elk, deer, and buffalo.

In Omaha, we stopped for *runzas* (beef and cabbage inside dough), Lithuanian pumpernickel bread, and *kolaches* (pastries).

The Sand Hills to the northwest are 20,000 square miles of grassy dunes and lakes. Every year the sandhill and whooping cranes gather on the Platte River. The sounds and sights make for another wild time in Nebraska.

Also wild here is football. The stadium at the University of Nebraska at Lincoln is larger than Yankee Stadium in New York City!

(a national holiday on which people plant trees) started in Nebraska.

The people who stayed in Nebraska were strong and healthy. They're the ones who didn't leave after all the droughts, plagues of grasshoppers, blizzards, and storms Nebraska has had.

Famous Cornhuskers (that means Nebraskans) include Fred Astaire, the dancer; former TV talk show host Johnny Carson, who did magic tricks in the small towns here; actor Marlon Brando; and writer Willa Cather, who grew up here. About Nebraska, she wrote: "As we drove further and further out into the [prairie] country, I felt a good deal as if we had come to the end of everything."

But maybe Nebraska is wilder than people

INTERESTING PLACE IN NEBRASKA

Boys Town was started on a farm near Omaha by Father Edward Flanagan as a home for troubled and homeless boys. Now 98 buildings are home to 500 boys *and* girls. Father Flanagan used to say: "There are no bad boys. There is only bad environment, bad training, bad example, bad thinking."

Colorado

It was a clear day when we drove into Colorado, and we could see mountains looming miles ahead of us. They seemed puny as we were driving along. But the closer we got, the more GIGANTIC they got. The Rocky Mountains mark the prairie's end, the official stop to the Midwest. It's said that "scenery is to Colorado what sunshine is to California."

Soon Grandma and I felt as tiny as Munchkins. In fact, you know what used to feel "at home" in Colorado? Dinosaurs! The remains of the largest, smallest, and oldest dinosaurs have all been found here. Colorado even has a state fossil: the stegosaurus.

This is the highest state, with more than half of the highest mountains in the lower 48 states. The most famous one is Pikes Peak, named for explorer Zebulon Pike. It was a big goal for the pioneers—that's where the expression "Pikes Peak or Bust" comes from.

We spent a day horseback riding at Rocky Mountain National Park. It's a wildlife sanctuary for bighorn sheep, elk, deer, and the fastest American mammal, the pronghorn antelope—which can run 40 miles per hour. The air is dry and pure.

After a day in the saddle (and I *didn't* fall off), we were beat. We had juicy steak for dinner, with sweet cantaloupe for dessert. We sat around a campfire and sang "I Ride an Old Paint" and "Git Along, Little Dogies." We pretended we were Butch Cassidy and the Sundance Kid, who used to hang out in Colorado. Then we unpacked our bedrolls and fell asleep under the stars.

Rocky Mountain National Park

CAPITAL: **Denver**

MOTTO: ***Nil Sine Numine*** (Nothing Without Providence)

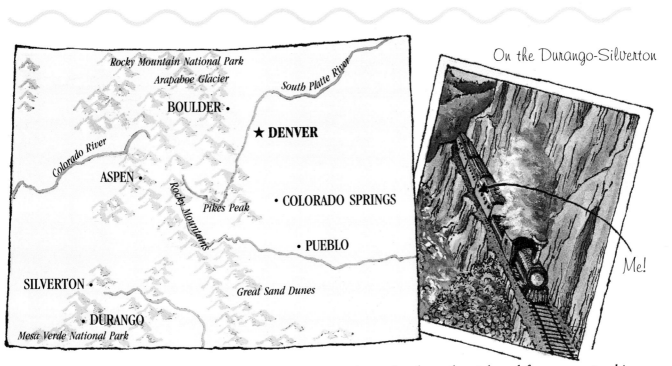

On the Durango-Silverton

Me!

Denver is called the Mile-High City because it's a mile above sea level. Too bad you can't always see the pretty views, because Denver is the second-smoggiest city in America. We visited the Denver Art Museum, with the largest collection of American Indian arts in the world, and the Black American West Museum, which honors black cowboys.

For breakfast, I had shredded wheat, a cereal invented in Denver. On the menu at dinner, I saw elk meat, rattlesnake, and buffalo burgers. I just ordered a burrito. Did you know that Denverites take more vitamins than people in any other city? It's a thrilling kind of place, with more sporting-goods stores per person than any other city. Softball was invented here.

Nearby Boulder gets its water from Arapahoe Glacier. It's the only city in North America that owns a glacier. Up the twisty mountain roads are more than 300 ghost towns left from Gold Rush and Wild West days.

Aspen is where the rich and famous go to ski in winter. Instead of snow, we saw something *hot:* sand—140 degrees in summer. (No going barefoot.) I'm talking about the Great Sand Dunes, the biggest desert sand dunes in North America. It took millions of years for the wind to make these smooth blond shapes, sometimes in heaps 700 feet high. To the Ute, the only American Indian people native to Colorado, this was a place full of gods and visions. Even today, legend has it that on full-moon nights, horses with webbed feet can be seen racing over the dunes. Wow!

The Great Sand Dunes

29

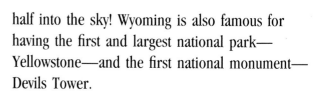

Wyoming

That's what the sign said as we entered the rectangle of Wyoming. Grandma was singing "Don't Fence Me In." She said this was the land of wide-open spaces, with some of the loneliest roads in America. But that doesn't mean ugly roads. Beartooth Highway here has been called "the most beautiful drive in America." It crosses Beartooth Pass with views of glaciers, snowcapped peaks, blue lakes, and rocky plateaus.

One cowboy we met told us there was less traffic now than there was during the pioneer days. Millions passed through here—on their way to other states. Wyoming's South Pass was famous as the easiest way to cross the mountains.

One good resting spot for weary wagon train travelers was Independence Rock, near Casper. We saw the names of thousands of those early pioneers, who carved their names into the rock here.

Wyoming, our second-highest state, is just as famous for mountains as Colorado is. The Tetons are the most steeply rising mountains in North America. The Grand Teton shoots a mile and a half into the sky! Wyoming is also famous for having the first and largest national park—Yellowstone—and the first national monument—Devils Tower.

Yellowstone is home to bears, waterfalls, and geysers, which are jets of superhot water from old volcanoes. The most famous geyser is Old Faithful: It faithfully spouts off about once an hour. We were sorry to miss Yellowstone in the fall, the mating season for 25,000 elk. Their mating call, which sounds something like bugles, is said to fill the whole park.

A bear!

Old Faithful, Yellowstone National Park

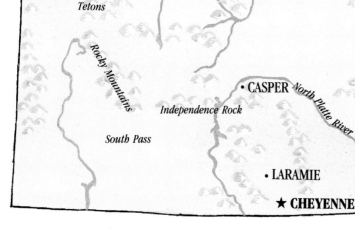

CAPITAL: **Cheyenne**
MOTTO: **Equal Rights**

Mount Moran in Grand Teton National Park

Devils Tower, looming in the Black Hills, was formed to help three little girls escape from angry bears, according to Sioux legend. Actually, I remembered this landmark from the movie *Close Encounters of the Third Kind*. It was the headquarters for the aliens from outer space.

The most popular event in Cheyenne is in late July—the famous Frontier Days, which includes one of the most important rodeos in the West. Now I know why the Wyoming license plate shows a cowboy on a bucking bronco. I do think Wyoming is the friendliest of all the states. Probably because they don't *see* too many people here. This state has the fewest people of all, with many more cattle and sheep than human beings.

WYOMING WOMEN

1. Women first permanently gained the vote in Wyoming—in 1869, before Wyoming was even a state.
2. Wyoming was the first state with a woman governor—Nellie Ross in 1925—and a woman justice of the peace—Esther Morris in 1879.
3. Women in Laramie were the first ones allowed to serve on a jury. In 1879, this was a very big deal, and newspaper reporters came from all over America to see it.

Independence Rock

31

Montana

Skipping stones at Avalanche Lake in Glacier National Park

Hundreds of millions of years ago, the place where we stood today was at the bottom of the sea. Over time, the layers of squishy mud and sand here hardened into rock. Earthquakes pushed the rock up, UP, and *UP.* Now Glacier National Park in Montana has mountains so steep that—get this—they've never been climbed. It also has 50 glaciers, which are rivers of ice, and hundreds of miles of trails.

Grandma and I drove along Going-to-the-Sun Road to the largest lake in the park—Lake McDonald. I can see why this is called the most beautiful 50-mile stretch of road in the world. We saw eagles and falcons, thousands of plants in bloom, and big trout jumping clear out of the water.

I think I know what people mean who say, "Montana is what America was." Grandma said that Montana is the greatest expanse of roadless country left in the United States, outside of Alaska. The wide-open spaces are home to birds and animals no longer found elsewhere. It's called Big Sky country, where the cattle outnumber people three to one.

After a breakfast of pancakes and bacon in Glendive, we searched in the dirt for pieces of the past to take home with us: arrowheads, or the tips from American Indian arrows. After all these years, there aren't many arrowheads left to find. Grandma was hoping we'd find a sapphire—Montana has more of these valuable gems than any other state. It also has huge deposits of copper, silver, coal, and gold. Even

CAPITAL: **Helena**

MOTTO: *Oro y Plata* **(Gold and Silver)**

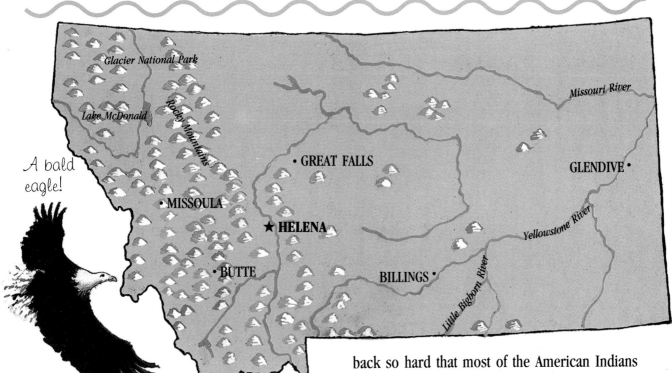

A bald eagle!

today, when a new building is built in Helena, diggers find gold dust.

Not too far away is where the Battle of the Little Bighorn took place, in 1876. This was one of the American Indians' last efforts to keep their land, and one of the most famous battles in our history. After General Custer and his troops were killed fighting Northern Cheyennes and Sioux, led by Chief Crazy Horse, white Americans fought

back so hard that most of the American Indians not yet on reservations were forced onto them.

We saw museums in almost every town, and old saddles and western gear for sale, and also rodeos. In one small town, we whooped and hollered as cowgirls and cowboys showed off their skills. No one knows where the first rodeo took place, but Grandma said it was probably when a bunch of cowboys decided to have a contest to see who was coolest. Being a cowboy was harder and more boring than most people think, and rodeos added some excitement. Today people who want to pretend to be cowboys (or who just love to ride horses) go to dude ranches, and Montana has more dude ranches than any other state.

The annual Crow Fair

FAMOUS MONTANANS

Charles M. Russell, the "Cowboy Artist," honored in Great Falls for his classic paintings of early western life. And Jeannette Rankin, from Missoula, the first woman elected to Congress, in 1916.

33

Idaho

For whom does the bell toll? It tolled for Grandma and me in Sun Valley, Idaho, where Ernest Hemingway wrote a book called *For Whom the Bell Tolls*. Now there's a famous resort here that attracts skiers from all over the world, including glittering movie stars.

More than 80 varieties of real gems are found within Idaho, and it's first in silver. In the Silver Valley, we took the Sierra Silver Mine tour. We put on hard hats and took a trailer down into a deep tunnel that stretches five blocks. Guides showed us how equipment is used today, and we got to take the little silver samples we found.

Whether they're mashed, french-fried, scalloped, or baked . . . Idaho is the leading potato state. It can grow 120 potatoes for every person in America! In fact, southeast Idaho is known as Famous Potato country. We saw green plants with yellow flowers; the actual potatoes are underground.

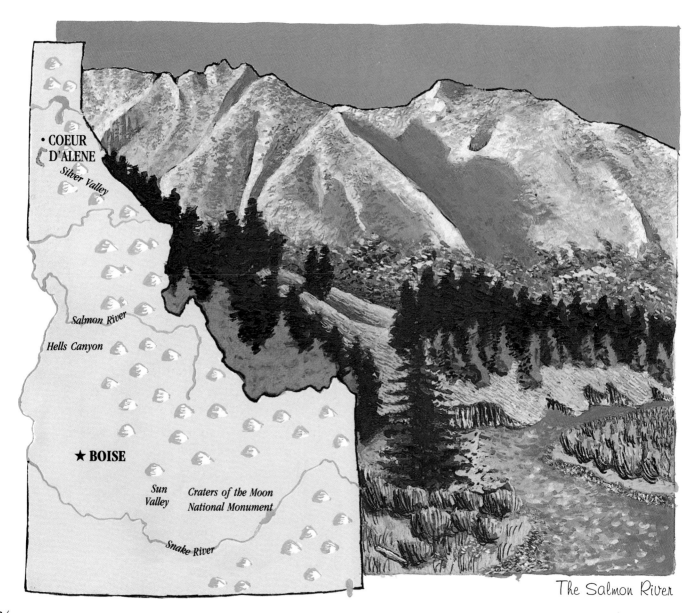

The Salmon River

COEUR D'ALENE

Silver Valley

Salmon River

Hells Canyon

★ BOISE

Sun Valley

Craters of the Moon National Monument

Snake River

CAPITAL: **Boise**

MOTTO: *Esto Perpetua* (It Is Perpetual)

Actually, we saw more mountains than potatoes in Idaho. It's *the* place for an outdoor life. Most people in Idaho live away from the cities. Many live near the Snake River. *In* the Snake River live sturgeon, the largest freshwater fish in America. Some weigh 1,000 pounds.

Riding the rapids

Hells Canyon on the Snake River is the deepest canyon in the world—7,900 feet deep. We drove a steep and winding road to a point called Heaven's Gate at Hells Canyon. Really! From there it was a short hike to a view of 150 varieties of wildflowers in bloom, and valleys full of bighorn sheep, bears, and cougars. The lakes here are good for fishing, but too cold for swimming.

The wild Salmon River is known as the river of no return. It roars downstream through the largest wilderness preserve in the lower 48 states. The only way upstream is by jet boat.

Another great place is Craters of the Moon National Monument. The multicolored lava here is

Craters of the Moon National Monument

the result of violent volcano eruptions over the past 15,000 years. Luckily, the volcanoes are extinct now. Seeing the spooky shapes in the craters is like being *on* the moon. Guess what? Astronauts going to the moon were given training here.

We stopped for fresh huckleberry ice cream and a concert in the park at Coeur d'Alene. This is said to be one of America's ten most livable towns, and its lake is said to be one of the five most beautiful on earth.

Maybe we should have saved Idaho for last, because this state was the last one to be seen by Europeans. Guided by Sacajawea, a Shoshone woman, Lewis and Clark arrived in 1805. But the Nez Percé were here first. Led by Chief Joseph, they fought hard in the 1870's against confinement on a reservation.

I can see why—Idaho is sensational country.

STRANGE IDAHO FACT

You can get a license to drive here when you're only 14. Just watch out for stray sheep and cattle on the road.

35

Washington

Queets Valley Rain Forest

Grandma and I were tiptoeing on a lush carpet of soft moss and licorice ferns. Above us hung a gorgeous green canopy of tall trees. We were in North America's only rain forest—Queets Valley Rain Forest in Washington's Olympic National Park. This jungle is one of the rainiest places in the world, full of rich soil and poisonous mushrooms! There are miles of trails here for people to walk on. But mainly this is a quiet, safe place for many kinds of animals and birds.

We had reached the states on the Pacific Ocean. Grandma said that the land along here is still moving around. To tell the truth, I think Mount Saint Helens is moving a little too much. The largest volcano eruption in America took place here in 1980. The sky filled with ashes and went dark. Lava spewed out of the mountaintop at 250 miles per hour. It killed plants, animals, and people, including scientists who had been studying the volcano since earthquakes started giving early warnings. Within a month, the ashes had traveled all the way around the world.

Washington is full of mountains and rivers. We got a sensational view from the top of the Space Needle at Seattle Center. The Cascade and Olympic Mountains are huge, and water and green trees are all around. Luckily, it was one of Seattle's clear days. This is the sixth-drizzliest place in America. When it rains, they say this is the slug capital of the country. But when it's *not* raining, some say this is the most beautiful city in America. We could hardly go in a straight line in Seattle, because a pretty lake or big hill was always in our way. Despite the rain, Seattleites buy more sunglasses per person than any other city dwellers in America. I could tell that this is a green city with water carnivals, boat races, and so much to do you could never get bored.

Bargaining at Seattle's Pike Place Market

CAPITAL: **Olympia**
MOTTO: *Alki* **(By and By)**

We put on our sunglasses and took a ferryboat journey all around Puget Sound. Almost 200 little islands dot the water. Some of them have no people at all on them. In the background was giant Mount Rainier, which has more than 25 glaciers. This is the snowiest spot in America.

This state is famous for seafood. I found out *why* the night we went to a salmon bake at the beach. It's also famous for crunchy red apples. Wenatchee ships more apples than any other city. But why do more people buy dieting magazines in Spokane than in any other American city? No one knows.

Fathers love Washington. It's the only state named after a president—the "Father" of our country. Maybe that's why Father's Day got started here—by Sonora Louise Smart Dodd of Spokane in 1909.

We left Grandma's little red car in Seattle and got on a plane for the next part of our grand Adventure!

From Grandma's Diary

Must send note to my publisher: More people check out library books in Seattle than in any other city in America. (Tacoma is a runner-up.)

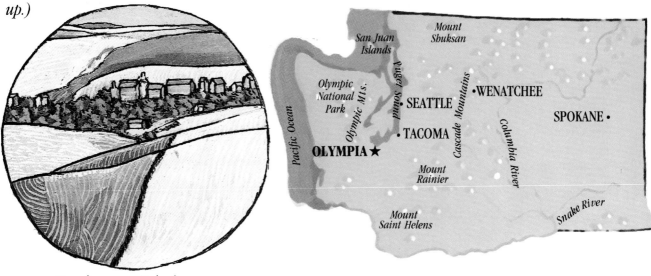

Southeastern Washington

Alaska

Isn't it weird that we have a state that's so far away?

I mean, part of Alaska is only two miles from Russia. Meanwhile, Washington—the nearest of the other states—is 500 miles away. In fact, America *bought* Alaska from Russia back in 1867, for about two cents an acre.

Grandma says Alaska is a land where nature is still wild. It has fewer miles of roads than tiny Vermont. She likes a book called *The Call of the Wild*, by Jack London. It's a classic adventure story set in Alaska.

All I know is that Alaska is HUGE. It has more than one million acres for each day of the year. The biggest state by far. But it has almost no people—just one person per square mile, and half of them live around Anchorage. Many Alaskans are Inuit, Aleuts, and American Indians such as the Athapascan and the Tlingit. Others are people who want to get rich from oil or fishing, or people who simply think Alaska is sensational.

Grandma said we didn't have time to see all 591,004 square miles of Alaska. So we went right to the top: We flew to Anchorage and took an air taxi to Mount McKinley. This is the highest mountain in North America—nearly four miles high. It is located in Denali National Park and Preserve, which is almost five million acres, bigger than Massachusetts!

Unfortunately, there were too many puffy clouds to see the mountain very well. Instead, we saw pure white Dall sheep; the largest moose in the world—try 1,500 pounds; sled dogs—dog mushing is the official state sport; my favorite animal, reindeer; and my *least* favorite, huge grizzly bears—try ten feet tall. Altogether there

Glacier Bay

are hundreds of kinds of birds and dozens of kinds of mammals here. All amid spectacular scenery and brilliant tundra wildflowers.

Bears, bears everywhere. We skipped Admiralty Island—one million acres, almost no roads, and 1,000 huge bears. Even in Juneau, the state capital, bears roam around just a short walk away from the capitol building.

For dinner back in Anchorage, Grandma had Alaskan king crab. I decided *against* a reindeer burger and had a peanut butter and salmonberry jelly sandwich instead.

CAPITAL: **Juneau**

MOTTO: **North to the Future**

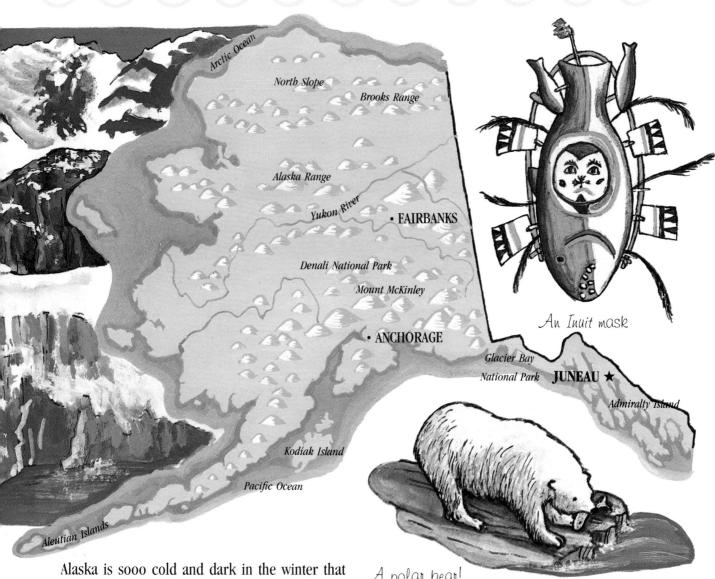

Arctic Ocean

North Slope

Brooks Range

Alaska Range

Yukon River

• FAIRBANKS

Denali National Park

Mount McKinley

• ANCHORAGE

Glacier Bay
National Park **JUNEAU** ★

Admiralty Island

Kodiak Island

Pacific Ocean

Aleutian Islands

An Inuit mask

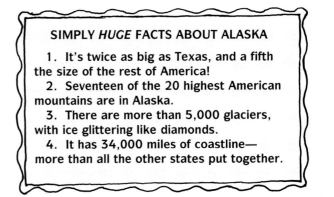

A polar bear!

Alaska is sooo cold and dark in the winter that people stay indoors for weeks on end. It can go as low as 75 degrees below zero. During blizzards, people hold on to strings between buildings to make sure they find their way. Cars get "square tires" after one side freezes flat to the ground.

The North Slope is called the land of the midnight sun. Every year it gets two months of constant summer sun, even at midnight.

Life in Alaska can certainly be tricky. But eeeks—was I sorry to leave.

SIMPLY *HUGE* FACTS ABOUT ALASKA

1. It's twice as big as Texas, and a fifth the size of the rest of America!
2. Seventeen of the 20 highest American mountains are in Alaska.
3. There are more than 5,000 glaciers, with ice glittering like diamonds.
4. It has 34,000 miles of coastline—more than all the other states put together.

Oregon

The Oregon coast

Back once again in the lower 48 (where all the states are except Alaska and Hawaii), Grandma and I got up extra early and walked along a

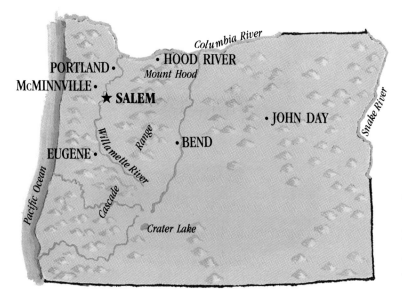

lonely white beach. The water was so cold it numbed my toes. We collected driftwood that was twisted into fantastic shapes and bleached by the pounding surf, and explored tidal pools for tiny sea creatures. Huge sea lions sunbathed on the rocks, barking and roaring every once in a while.

We were in Oregon, the Pacific Wonderland, a place that makes me feel healthy just thinking about it. Backpacking, river rafting, skiing, and camping are all within easy reach of Oregon's cities. Its coastline has been called the most scenic marine border in the world. Oregon has many laws to make sure it stays that way.

That night we went to a smelt fry. This coast is famous for smelt, those tiny silver fish that you have to eat a lot of to get full. For dessert we had wild blackberry pie.

Portland is the cloudiest city in America, but

CAPITAL: **Salem**

MOTTO: *Alis Volat Propriis* **(She Flies with Her Own Wings)**

Mount Hood

when it's clear it's one of the prettiest. We saw magical Mount Hood just outside the city, as well as rose gardens everywhere. This is the City of Roses; one of the largest children's parades in America takes place during its Rose Festival. This is also the river city. The Willamette River, full of water-skiers and salmon-fishers, divides the city in half.

At the World Forestry Center, we saw a talking tree (not real) and learned about the forest. Oregon has blankets of Douglas fir—a tree that takes eighty years to grow up. This is said to be the best region in the world for high-quality timber. Millions of ships and houses are made with Oregon wood.

Windsurfing on the Hood River

The nearby city of Hood River calls itself the windsurfing capital of the world. Watching the colorful sails bouncing on the waves, we got hungry again. Grandma had salmon, while I had slumgullion, a creamy shrimp stew.

Oregon smells nice. Parts are full of peppermint farms, and also apple and pear orchards. In a town called John Day, we visited the Kam Wah Chung & Co. Museum. The majority of people in

eastern Oregon used to be Chinese, and this was their trading post. Now it's full of Chinese herbs, toys, and furniture. Today, Oregon ranks fourth for resettling refugees from Asia.

Oregon has the deepest, bluest lake in America. Crater Lake, on top of a dead volcano, was a sacred place for the Klamath people. The lake traps most of the sun's rays, leaving the pure blue rays to reflect back up through the clear water. Very mysterious!

WRITING IN OREGON

1. Beverly Cleary was born in McMinnville. All her great stories about Ramona Quimby and Henry Huggins take place in a Portland suburb.

2. James Stevens worked as a logger in Bend. No wonder he wrote a collection of tall tales about champion logger Paul Bunyan, and also a funny folk song called "The Frozen Logger."

A poppy farm, Willamette Valley

California

"Everything worth photographing is in California," said the famous photographer Edward Weston. One out of nine Americans must agree—that's who lives in this, our most populated state. About one-fourth of them can speak a language other than English.

California is too much—the third-largest state, to be exact. It has so much sunshine, good soil for farming, and money that many people think of it as a promised land. For sure, only good things happened to me and Grandma. We worked on our tans, watched surfers, went to a beach party, and ate oranges and grapes. California produces more of our food than any other state.

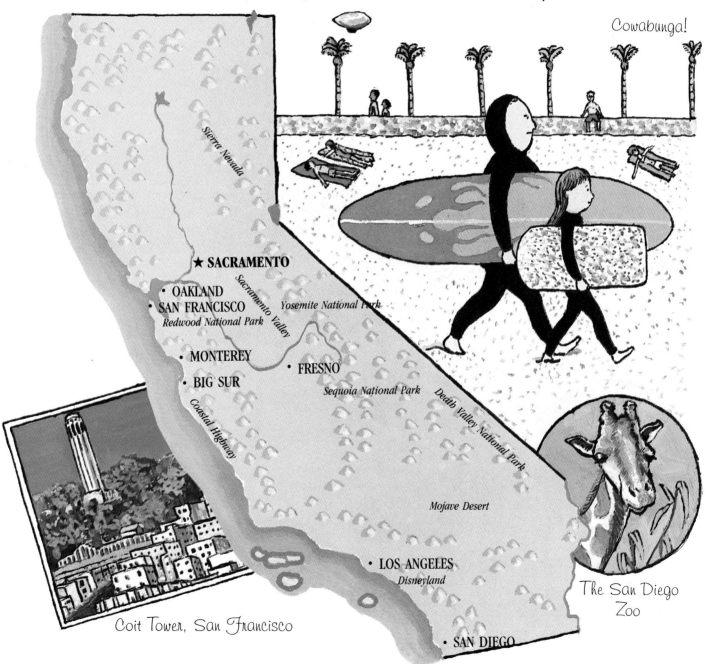

Cowabunga!

Sierra Nevada

★ SACRAMENTO

• OAKLAND
• SAN FRANCISCO
Redwood National Park

Sacramento Valley

Yosemite National Park

• MONTEREY
• BIG SUR

• FRESNO

Sequoia National Park

Death Valley National Park

Coastal Highway

Mojave Desert

• LOS ANGELES
Disneyland

Coit Tower, San Francisco

The San Diego Zoo

• SAN DIEGO

We decided that if there was a Most Beautiful City in America contest, hilly San Francisco would get our vote. Try 40 hills. We rode the cable cars, ate Ghirardelli chocolates, and drove over the Golden Gate Bridge.

And for scariest drive, we vote for the Coastal Highway that took us down the West Coast. It's a giant roller coaster, with jagged cliffs that made my heart beat fast (Grandma's, too). She said Robert Louis Stevenson modeled his settings in *Treasure Island* after the Big Sur and Monterey area along here.

We shoot a flick

Los Angeles—if you're cool you say "L.A."—is where all of my favorite TV shows and movies are made, and everyone else's, too. Hmm, maybe that's why L.A. County has more millionaires than any other county in America. Near L.A. is Disneyland, where I went on *all* the rides, and Mattel, Inc., where a woman once invented dolls she named after her daughter and son, Barbie and Ken. Guess who lived in the town called Tarzana: Edgar Rice Burroughs, who wrote the Tarzan books!

San Diego is next to Mexico, with the most heavily traveled border in the world. It's *balmy* all year round. I guess that's why every ten min-utes one more person moves here. We saw beautiful flowers with strange names. Besides the miles of beaches and bike paths, the best part of the city is the zoo. It's the world's largest—try 3,400 animals. Even Grandma went ape there. Ha ha ha! Second-best place is the Hotel del Coronado, a sensational castle that inspired L. Frank Baum in writing *The Wizard of Oz.*

I guess California isn't *always* perfect. Los Angeles has smog—and way too many cars and freeways. Earthquakes can shake things up here—scientists think there will be a major, heavy-duty earthquake before the year 2006. But till *that* happens, I'll still keep dreaming California dreams.

Or maybe Hawaiian dreams . . . ?

A FEW WORDS ABOUT CALIFORNIA'S TREES

1. We saw PALM TREES. Truly the weirdest thing I noticed about California.
2. The tallest trees in the world are the redwoods in Redwood National Park.
3. In Sequoia National Park is the most massive living thing in the world: General Sherman, a giant sequoia 275 feet tall.
4. The oldest known living tree in the world is Methuselah, a bristlecone pine in the White Mountains—try 4,600 years old.

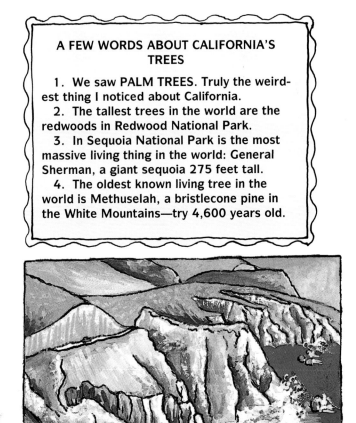

The Coastal Highway on the Monterey Peninsula   43

Hawaii

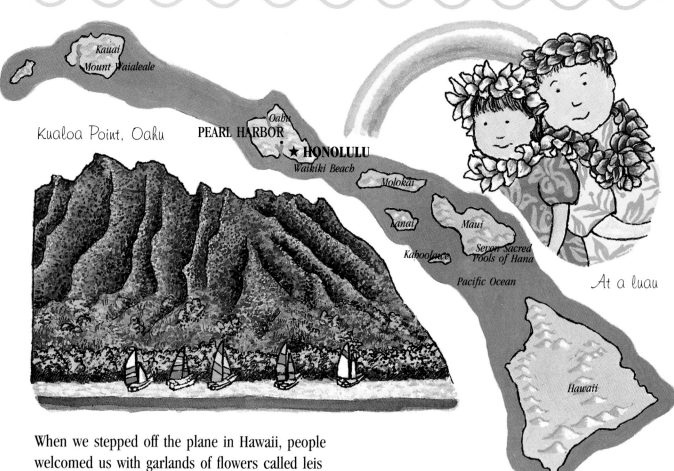

Kualoa Point, Oahu

Kauai
Mount Waialeale

Oahu
PEARL HARBOR
★ HONOLULU
Waikiki Beach

Molokai

Lanai

Maui
Seven Sacred
Pools of Hana

Kahoolawe

Pacific Ocean

At a luau

Hawaii

When we stepped off the plane in Hawaii, people welcomed us with garlands of flowers called leis and shouts of *"Aloha!"*

If you ask people what heaven is like, a lot of them will say "Hawaii." More than 2,000 miles from California, Hawaii is the only state not even in North America. It's also the only state made up of islands. It has 132. Only eight of them are large enough for people to live on.

The big island of Hawaii is the southernmost point in the United States, believe it or not. Here, the world's largest active volcano erupts every few years. When the ocean cools the lava, it becomes hard and makes the island bigger. Most people live on another island, Oahu, home to Honolulu and wild Waikiki Beach. Iolani Palace is the only royal palace in America—Hawaii used to have kings and queens! Grandma said that the Japa-nese bombing of Pearl Harbor, a military base here, brought America into World War II.

Molokai has the highest sea cliffs in the world, stretching 3,300 feet down to the Pacific Ocean. Kauai contains the wettest place on earth—Mount Waialeale gets more than 38 feet of rain a year. Off Kauai is the "forbidden island" of Niihau, where no visitors are allowed. Native Hawaiians preserve the old ways here. According to legend, this is the home of the fire goddess Pele. Visitors are not allowed at Kahoolawe either, because it's used for military target practice. Another island, Lanai, has the world's largest pineapple plan-tation.

Grandma and I spent most of our time on

CAPITAL: **Honolulu**

MOTTO: *Ua Mau Ke Ea O Ka Aina I Ka Pono*
(The Life of the Land Is Perpetuated in Righteousness)

Maui, an island with 33 miles of beaches, some of black volcanic ash, some golden. Kids *and* grown-ups surf here—surfing was invented by the ancient kings of Hawaii. A roller-coaster drive over mountain roads—wheee!—took us to the Seven Sacred Pools of Hana. A gorgeous waterfall splashed nearby. The air was the sweetest I've ever breathed. Peacocks walked right up to me. Suddenly a warm, gentle rain fell. When it stopped, a rainbow sparkled across the sky.

Nearly everything grows in Hawaii, including sugarcane, mangoes, papayas, bananas, guavas, and passion fruit. It's the only state that grows coffee. The brightest flowers grow year-round—most of them exist nowhere else.

That night we went to a luau, a traditional feast where food is cooked in a pit over hot stones. We drank coconut juice and ate roast pork, vegetables wrapped in banana leaves, and poi—a native dish made of cooked taro root. Women played ukuleles and did the native dance of Hawaii—the hula, which tells a story with the hands.

Hawaii, our newest state, is the only one where the roots of the majority are Asian or Pacific Islander (Japanese, Chinese, Filipino), not European. The Polynesian language, native to Hawaii, gets its musical sound from having only 12 letters. Muumuus are the long loose dresses I saw many women wearing here.

Did you know that people live longer lives in Hawaii than in any other state? It does cost a lot to live here, and some parts are too touristy. But if you asked *me* what heaven is like, I'd say "Hawaii."

The Seven Sacred Pools of Hana, Maui

45

Nevada

Guess where we landed next. A state that has many more marriages (and divorces) than any other. The only place that allows gambling throughout the whole state. A small population, but enough visitors to outnumber most other states. Nevada? Right.

Nevada gets less rain than any other state, but it wasn't a total desert the way I thought it was going to be. It's half mountain, half valley. Long ago, there were even lakes here, but unfortunately they're dead lakes now. Most pioneers going to California passed through Nevada as fast as they could.

Death Valley, for example, is the lowest and hottest place in America. Even its name makes me sweaty. It's partly in California but seems more Nevada-like. Amazingly, several kinds of rare fish live in Death Valley. In this strange and eerie landscape, hot springs run into cool mountain streams. You can catch a fish in one and cook it in the other!

One highway across the middle of Nevada is called the loneliest road in America. For long, lonely stretches, all you see is sagebrush. Mark Twain called sagebrush "the ugliest plant ever." But I liked its gray-green color and its special perfume in the night.

We drive the loneliest road in America

RENO
• VIRGINIA CITY
★ CARSON CITY
Lake Tahoe

Great Basin

PIOCHE •

• GOLDFIELD

Death Valley National Park
LAS VEGAS
• Hoover Dam

Colorado River

In Pioche, the site of a silver mine, people told us that it used to be one tough town—so lawless that none of the first 70 men in its cemetery died "in their beds." Towns like this call their cemeteries Boot Hill after men who died violently, or "with their boots on."

Virginia City is the site of the Comstock Lode, probably the richest single mine ever discovered—it turned ordinary people into multimillionaires. There's no gold and silver left now, just me and Grandma. Visitors like us are important to Nevada now. Almost one out of ten Americans vacations in Las Vegas annually.

Know why Las Vegas has the highest electric bills in America—by far? Because of its air-conditioning, and its neon lights that flash all night long. The most photographed things in Las Vegas are a neon cowboy and cowgirl—try 60 feet high. Las Vegas is the gambling capital of America—the place where adults can play games of chance in which it's possible to win (and lose) money. More than half the people in Nevada live around Las Vegas (if you're cool you call it Vegas). And almost 400 people *a day* get married here.

Las Vegas has more entertainers (dancers, showgirls, musicians, and composers) per person than any other city. It's the live-entertainment capital of America. At the Liberace Museum, we saw fancy costumes this entertainer used to wear, and all his glittery pianos and cars. This is the perfect, show-offy Las Vegas kind of place. Lots of rhinestones and sequins.

Virginia City

NEVADA NUGGET

Nevada has the highest percentage of houses built after 1950. This is our fastest-growing state.

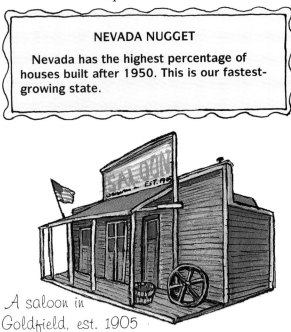

A saloon in Goldfield, est. 1905

47

Utah

Grandma and I riding shotgun in Monument Valley

"Howdy, pardner. I mean, Grandma."

We were in Kanab, Utah. So many westerns and TV shows have been filmed in these parts that this area is known as Little Hollywood. Some of these flat-topped mountains and canyons looked mighty familiar. In Moab, we went to the Hollywood Stuntmen's Hall of Fame. Movie clips show off the brave people who actually perform the dangerous stunts that the stars pretend to do.

Utah is where you go if you love rocks. It has more red rock country than any other state—that means red sandstone carved by wind and rain into formations of all kinds. Take the longest natural bridge in the world, the Landscape Arch in Arches National Park near Moab. This park has *thousands* of arches, formed bit by bit over millions of years. Foxes and jackrabbits live here, as well as coyotes, bobcats, and even mountain lions. At night the bats come out, and also

desert lizards, some of them a foot long.

I can see why so many artists live around here, painting the red rock country—pictures of it, I mean. Pictures have been part of life here since the petroglyphs, or rock carvings, created by the Anasazi, or Ancient Ones.

Bryce Canyon has some of the most colorful rocks on earth—red, pink, cream, lavender. On the floor of the canyon here are ponderosa pine trees. They smell like butterscotch! But here's the really wild part: Because of erosion, the rocks keep shaping and reshaping themselves over time . . . into forms that look like people, animals, castles, or whatever your imagination can think of. Some of the forms have names, like Fairyland, Queen's Garden, the Cathedral, Silent City, Aqua Canyon, Pink Cliffs—you get the idea of what these places look like.

And you should see the lakes—Utah has the

CAPITAL: Salt Lake City

MOTTO: Industry

largest body of water in between the Great Lakes and the Pacific Ocean. I took a taste of the Great Salt Lake—and spit it right out! Streams full of minerals flow into this lake, leaving salt behind to make this the saltiest lake in America. It can be as much as eight times saltier than the ocean. No wonder Salt Lake City smells salty, just the way an ocean city does. There are even seagulls here, far from either coast.

In the Tabernacle at Temple Square in Salt Lake City, we heard the famous Mormon Tabernacle Choir and its gigantic organ. The choir's Sunday radio broadcast is the oldest continuous radio program in America. The majority of Utahans are Mormons, or members of the Church of Jesus Christ of Latter-day Saints.

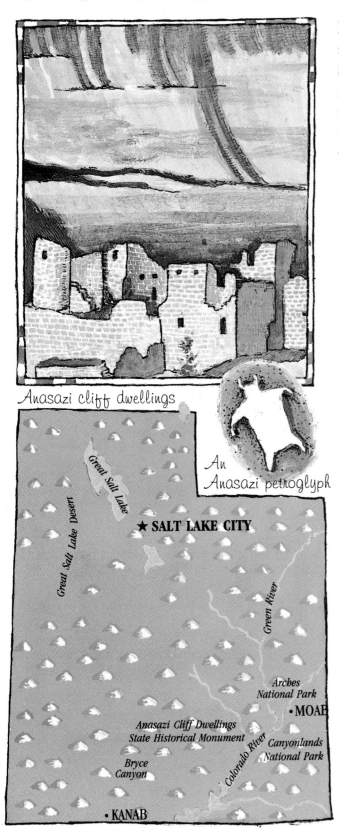

Anasazi cliff dwellings

An Anasazi petroglyph

Great Salt Lake Desert

Great Salt Lake

★ SALT LAKE CITY

Green River

Arches National Park

• MOAB

Anasazi Cliff Dwellings State Historical Monument

Colorado River

Canyonlands National Park

Bryce Canyon

• KANAB

ODD UTAH FACTS

1. Utahans eat more candy bars, Jell-O, hot cereal, and marshmallows than do people in any other state. But Utah still ties with Hawaii for having the least number of overweight people!

2. Utah has more kids under ten than any other state. (And kids here spend more years in school than in any other state.)

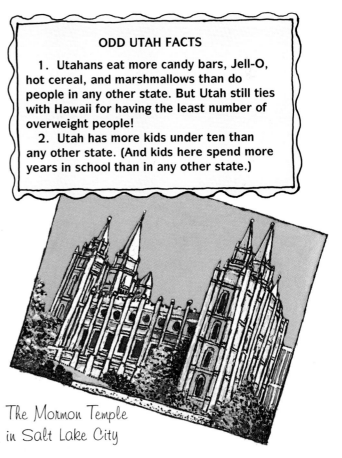

The Mormon Temple in Salt Lake City

Arizona

A Gila monster

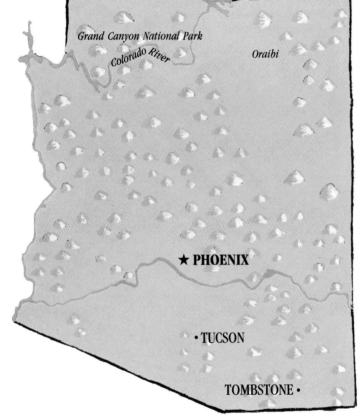

Trekking at the Grand Canyon

idea! Phoenix has 300 sunny days a year, which explains the 1,000 tennis courts and 90 golf courses. Tucson has more telescopes than any-where—it's the astronomy capital of the world.

For lunch we went to a steakhouse with saw-dust all over the floor. Grandma had a giant T-bone steak. I had a plate of cowboy beans. The jukebox played a twangy song about broken hearts. All around us were people wearing cowboy hats, Levi's, cowboy boots, long-sleeved western-style shirts, and bola ties. One cowboy told us that Arizona was once thought a useless desert. But now it's one of the fastest-growing states, thanks to air-conditioning.

Mountain peaks were everywhere we looked. So were cacti. There's the saguaro cactus (the largest cactus in America—try 50 feet high), stretching its arms up to the bright blue sky. One cactus *jumped* at me when I walked by. Yes, it was a *jumping* cactus—sensitive to movement. Be sure not to steal any cacti—you can go to jail! Cacti don't grow very fast, and some kinds

"When you call me that—*smile!*" I was practic-ing my best cowboy lines in Tombstone, Arizona, where we stopped for tall frosty mugs of sarsapa-rilla—a drink something like root beer. This is "the town too tough to die," where Wyatt Earp won fame as a gunfighter at the O.K. Corral.

Arizona is *hot,* dusty, and dry. The sun was so bright it hurt my eyes. And don't try walking down the street in your bare feet—ouch, bad

CAPITAL: **Phoenix**

MOTTO: *Ditat Deus* **(God Enriches)**

are becoming extinct because too many people are stealing them.

The desert is home to 37 kinds of lizards, including poisonous Gila monsters—ugh. We saw a few javelina, which is a kind of wild pig, and a few dust devils, or miniature whirlwind sandstorms.

One in 20 Arizonans is an American Indian, mostly Navajo and Hopi, plus 11 other tribes. The Hopi built the village of Oraibi 800 years ago and have been there since. For a souvenir, I bought a Hopi kachina doll.

Well, I've seen pictures of it, but the Grand Canyon is something else in person. It's a gorge 277 miles long and a mile deep. In other words, a big hole in the ground . . . that happens to be one of the Seven Natural Wonders of the World. Theodore Roosevelt called it "the one great sight every American should see." We spent a whole day riding mules down to the Colorado River at the canyon floor and back again. Guess what— the river acts like sandpaper, making the canyon the tiniest bit bigger even as I watched. I lost my breath at the sight of rock walls in dazzling orange and yellow and at least 12 shades of red. The oldest rock layers date back two *billion* years! Just how old Grandma said she felt the next day, with all her sore muscles.

JUDGING ARIZONA

Arizona Judge Sandra Day O'Connor was the first woman to be appointed to the Supreme Court of the United States, in 1981. Arizona Judge Lorna Lockwood was the first woman elected to head a state supreme court, in 1965.

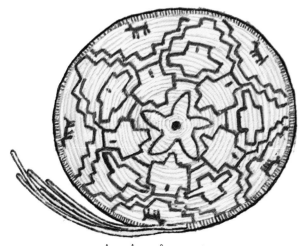

An Apache basket

New Mexico

Shiprock

So much space, so few people. Not Mexico, but *New* Mexico, where you can drive for hours without seeing another car, just the electric blue color of the sky. I never saw such a big sky, the wind blowing without anything to get in its way. Distant mountains glowed like blue pearls, changing to reds and purples as the sun set.

Near Socorro, we took dirt roads to explore prehistoric ruins and ghost towns. Grandma said that for thousands of years before Columbus reached America, many people have called New Mexico home—the ancient Anasazi, and the Pueblo, Apache, and Navajo. Next came Spanish and Mexican settlers (this has the highest percentage of Spanish-speaking residents of any state), then cowboys and adventurers. It's weird to think that history goes back further here than in any other state. The oldest American road is El Camino Real, which means the Royal Highway. It was built in 1581 by Spain. The oldest public building in America is Santa Fe's Palace of the Governors.

- TAOS PUEBLO
LOS ALAMOS •
★ SANTE FE
• ALBUQUERQUE
Rio Grande
Pecos River
SOCORRO •
White Sands National Monument
Carlsbad Caverns National Park

San Miguel Mission, oldest church in the U.S.A.

CAPITAL: **Santa Fe**

MOTTO: *Crescit Eundo* **(It Grows as It Goes)**

Taos Pueblo, inhabited since the 1200s

New Mexico is the land of enchantment for artists. Early American Indian artists carved their works into rock. Painters like Georgia O'Keeffe were inspired by bleached bones on the sparse landscape. Now Santa Fe is the center for southwestern art, with many museums and artists' studios.

In Santa Fe, we had chips with salsa, and sopapillas with honey. Also blue corn enchiladas, roasted piñon nuts, and dishes based on either red or green chili peppers. Whew—spicy. If you want both colors, you say "Christmas, please!" For dessert, Grandma had puddinglike flan, and I had cactus candy. I loved the narrow, winding cobblestone streets of Santa Fe, the Spanish gardens, and the red chili *ristras* hanging on the front doors of the adobe (sun-dried brick) houses. In Old Town, I bought Grandma a Pueblo figure of little children clinging to a wise old storyteller.

Grandma's storyteller doll

More than one-third of New Mexicans live around Albuquerque. Its International Hot Air Balloon Fiesta is the most photographed event in the world.

Water is hard to find in New Mexico. Try the underground fairyland at Carlsbad Caverns National Park, the largest group of connected caves ever discovered. Water drips down and mixes with minerals to create bright colors.

A place with *no* color is the White Sands National Monument. These pure white rippling gypsum sand dunes can move around so fast you have to watch where you park your car. Look out for roadrunners, the state birds.

White Sands

MOST SERIOUS PLACES IN NEW MEXICO

New Mexico is a leading center for space and nuclear research. In fact, Los Alamos was built to be a center for atomic research. The first atomic bomb was tested in July 1945 at Trinity Site at the White Sands Missile Range, near Jornada del Muerto, or Journey of Death. A month later, America dropped atomic bombs on Hiroshima and Nagasaki, destroying most of these two cities in Japan, during the final days of World War II.

53

Texas

They say Texas folk hero Pecos Bill used a hurricane to fan himself, and he rode around on the back of a tornado—for fun.

I guess everything just seems bigger in Texas—the tall tales, sun, horses, people's smiles, their cowboy hats, and the state itself. Until Alaska came along, Texas was our biggest state. Depending on where you're standing, you could be in the Gulf Coastal Plains (the eastern area where oil and chemical industries are based), the Piney Woods (the northeastern part of the plain), the Rio Grande Valley (and its fertile farms), the Central Plains (a rolling prairie), the triangular desert to the west, a lovely city (like Austin), or the hot High Plains (where the Texas Panhandle is). That's a lot of elbowroom.

This is the state with the most cattle and sheep, the most farms, and the most farmers. Grandma said that Texas's riches stretch from underground, with oil and natural gas, all the way to outer space. In fact, "Houston" was the first word ever said on the moon. Astronaut Neil Armstrong was talking to the Johnson Space Center in Houston—the headquarters for NASA projects with astronauts, named for Lyndon B. Johnson, a president from Texas.

Home on the range!

The Dallas–Fort Worth area is a perfect example of Texas variety. Dallas, they say, is where the East ends. To us it seemed like one glittery skyscraper after another. In Fort Worth, where they say the "real" West begins, we did notice a lot of people in cowboy boots. We went to a cattle auction in the Stockyards National Historic District. Grandma told me to be sure to keep my hands down, so I didn't buy any cattle by mistake!

Back on the road, we saw miles of bluebonnet flowers. Texas has more kinds of wildflowers than any other state. Keeping an eye out for armadillos, we saw hills covered with the purple haze of sage in bloom. I don't know how many trucks we saw—Texas has more pickup trucks than any other state.

CAPITAL: **Austin**
MOTTO: **Friendship**

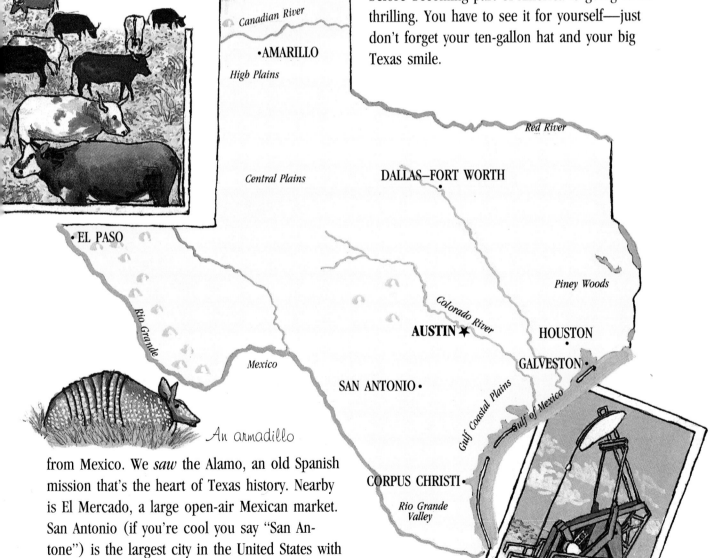

Soon we were floating down the San Antonio River in a water taxi. The Paseo del Rio, or River-walk, runs through San Antonio, with bridges and plenty of magnolias. And who could forget the Alamo? "Remember the Alamo!" is one of the most famous battle cries in American history—what Sam Houston's troops yelled as he led them to a final victory in winning Texan independence

from Mexico. We *saw* the Alamo, an old Spanish mission that's the heart of Texas history. Nearby is El Mercado, a large open-air Mexican market. San Antonio (if you're cool you say "San An-tone") is the largest city in the United States with a Hispanic majority.

We ate fajitas, or steamed tortillas filled with meat, peppers, and onions. Other famous Texas foods are Dr Pepper, invented in Waco as a cough syrup; cactus jelly; chili, which some say was invented as a spicy way to disguise bad meat in jail; and lots of beef dishes, especially with tangy barbecue sauce.

I could tell tall tales about Texas forever. Any state that was its own *country* for ten years before becoming part of America is going to be thrilling. You have to see it for yourself—just don't forget your ten-gallon hat and your big Texas smile.

An armadillo

Canadian River

•AMARILLO

High Plains

Red River

Central Plains

DALLAS–FORT WORTH

•EL PASO

Piney Woods

Rio Grande

Colorado River

AUSTIN ★

HOUSTON

Mexico

GALVESTON•

SAN ANTONIO •

Gulf Coastal Plains

Gulf of Mexico

CORPUS CHRISTI•

Rio Grande Valley

Oil!

55

Oklahoma

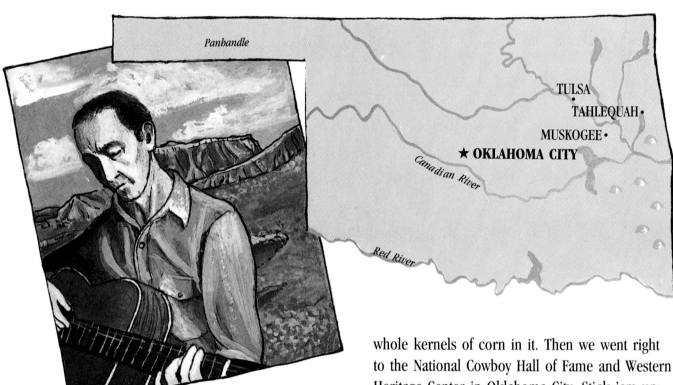

Woody Guthrie, 1912–67

"'This land is my land,'" we sang loudly as we rolled into the land of the tumbling tumbleweeds.

Grandma said that Woody Guthrie, her favorite folksinger, was from Oklahoma. He wrote "This Land Is Your Land," which some people think is America's theme song, and hundreds of other great songs. What a musical state. The state song is "Oklahoma!" from the Broadway musical of the same name. "Oklahoma, O.K.!"

Oklahoma wasn't the dry, dusty place I thought it would be. In fact, its lakes give it more shoreline than the East and Gulf Coasts combined. It's shaped like a rectangle, except for that strip hanging over Texas. Notice how that looks like the handle of a pan? Hmm, wonder why this part of Oklahoma is called the Panhandle!

We stopped for a snack of cornbread with whole kernels of corn in it. Then we went right to the National Cowboy Hall of Fame and Western Heritage Center in Oklahoma City. Stick 'em up: This is the world's largest museum devoted to the Old West. I liked the giant map with lights showing the routes cowboys took across America.

Oklahoma's "black gold" is oil, and you can become a millionaire overnight if you discover oil in your backyard. Oklahoma City is right on top of oil fields. One well tower even sits in front of the state capitol building. Tulsa calls itself the oil capital of the world.

Black gold at the State Capitol

56

CAPITAL: **Oklahoma City**

MOTTO: ***Labor Omnia Vincit*** **(Labor Conquers All Things)**

A Creek man in traditional clothing

Near Tulsa is Tahlequah, where we visited the Cherokee Heritage Center, which shows the history of this people since prehistoric times. Oklahoma was once considered such an out-of-the-way place that the American government used to banish American Indians here from the South. Now Oklahoma, with more than 60 peoples, is a major center of American Indian culture.

Will Rogers, the cowboy philosopher and the highest-paid Hollywood star of his time, was from Oklahoma. He was the one who said, "If you don't like the weather in Oklahoma, just wait a minute; it'll change." Once he was asked by a stuffy New Englander if his family had come over on the *Mayflower.* He said, "No, ma'am, but we met the boat." He was part Cherokee.

This is a state where what you've accomplished lately is more important than who your family is. Oklahoma has a blustery, macho image. But there must be kissing here, too: The mistletoe is the state flower!

NICKNAMES

Oklahomans were called Okies during the 1930's Depression. Dust storms killed cattle and crops, and families fled the state. There are many photographs of those Okies, and a famous book, too: *The Grapes of Wrath* by John Steinbeck, about a family lured to California by the promise of jobs picking fruit. In the 1960's, Oklahoma's governor said that "Okie" stood for "Oklahoma, Key to Industrial Expansion." And by 1970, the No. 1 song in America was Merle Haggard's "Okie from Muskogee," which was about being proud to be an Okie.

Lake Country

Kansas

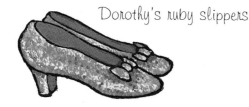
Dorothy's ruby slippers

"My name is *not* Toto," Grandma kept saying. "And we *are* in Kansas."

That's because *I* kept saying, "Toto, I don't think we're in Kansas anymore!" It's what Dorothy said to her dog in *The Wizard of Oz,* of course.

Kansas is the sort of flat, peaceful place where it looks as if nothing might happen. Kansas makes Oz seem even wilder than it is. But Kansas wind can be wild: It's a *very* popular state for tornadoes to start up. Remember the tornado in *The Wizard of Oz*?

Kansas is all rolling hills, golden with wheat, corn, and sunflowers. Kansas produces more wheat than any other state. Actually, wheat grew poorly here till a religious group called the Mennonites brought in a winter wheat from Russia. Now Kansas is known as the breadbasket of America.

Near Kansas City is the Agricultural Hall of Fame—270 acres in honor of the hardworking farmer and inventors like George Washington Carver, Eli Whitney, and Cyrus McCormick. This is the greatest collection of agricultural equipment in America—plus a whole reconstructed town from the olden days.

La Crosse has an entire museum in honor of . . . barbed wire. Why? Well, this one invention changed the history of the entire Great Plains. It allowed ranchers to keep their cattle *in* and danger *out*. The Barbed Wire Museum has more than 500 varieties, if you can imagine.

We stopped for fresh warm bread in Wichita, once an important point on the Chisholm Trail for cattle on their way to Kansas railroads. Kansas was once the largest cattle market in the world. Even today, many people think Kansas beef tastes the best. Now more than half the civilian airplanes in America are built in Wichita. What a coincidence, since Amelia Earhart, the pioneering aviator, came from Kansas.

Dodge City used to be the cowboy capital of America. It was a classic Wild West town where Bat Masterson, Wyatt Earp, and Wild Bill Hickok tried to keep law and order. Nearby, Finney

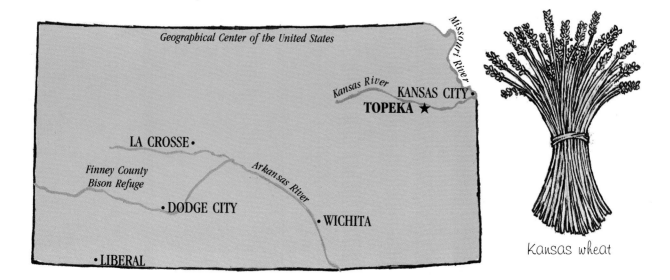

Geographical Center of the United States

Missouri River

Kansas River KANSAS CITY

TOPEKA ★

LA CROSSE

Finney County Bison Refuge

Arkansas River

• DODGE CITY

• WICHITA

• LIBERAL

Kansas wheat

CAPITAL: **Topeka**

MOTTO: *Ad Astra per Aspera*
(To the Stars Through Difficulties)

Grandma about to rope a calf

Wild Bill Hickok

County Bison Refuge shelters a small buffalo herd. Huge hairy beasts grazed on tall bluestem grass and sage. We rode in a pickup truck and took a picture of them. I didn't want to get too close—buffalo can be moody!

Grandma told me that Great Plains buffalo used to number around 70 million. Now bison refuges like this one hold some of the few thousand buffalo left. "Buffalo Bill" Cody got his name in Kansas, from shooting a record number of buffalo to feed railroad workers.

"Oh, give me a home where the buffalo roam . . ." Did you know that "Home on the Range" was the state song of Kansas?

Surely, we never heard "a discouraging word" while we were there.

WILDEST THING ABOUT KANSAS

There are *two* cities named Kansas City. One is in Kansas. Okay. But the other, bigger one is in next-door neighbor *Missouri*!

Tornado!

59

Missouri

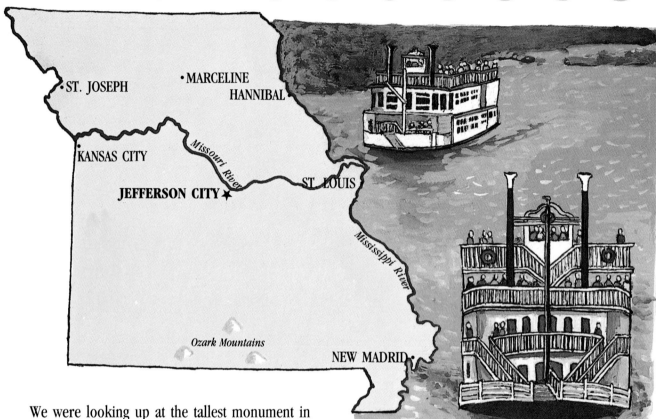

The annual
Great Riverboat Race on the Missouri River

We were looking up at the tallest monument in the world and eating ice-cream cones at the same time. Grandma told me about a girl who once got flowers and an ice-cream sandwich from her boyfriend. She took the top wafer of the sandwich and wrapped it around the flowers as a vase. She wrapped the other wafer around the ice cream to keep it from dripping. She had invented the first ice-cream cone! It was 1904, at the world's fair in St. Louis, Missouri. Introduced at the same fair were the hamburger, the hot dog, and iced tea.

And the tallest monument? It's the Gateway Arch in St. Louis—try 630 feet of shimmering steel dominating the skyline. We sang "Meet Me in St. Louis" and "St. Louis Blues" as we looked up.

Most people in Missouri live around St. Louis or Kansas City. T. S. Eliot was from St. Louis; he wrote *Old Possum's Book of Practical Cats* and

lots of other famous poems. Kansas City was home to Thomas Hart Benton, once America's best-known painter. This used to be known as

Listening to jazz in Kansas City

CAPITAL: **Jefferson City**
MOTTO: ***Salus Populi Suprema Lex Esto***
**(The Welfare of the People Shall Be the
Supreme Law)**

"the most lawless city in America." Now it's famous for Kansas City–style jazz music.

Mail must be important in Missouri. Hallmark Cards come from the world's largest greeting card company, in Kansas City. And St. Joseph was the starting place for the Pony Express in 1860 and 1861, when it took riders ten days to get the mail from there to San Francisco.

We "let off steam" during a ride on a riverboat called *Mark Twain.* That expression comes from relieving a steamboat's boiler pressure through a valve. We were in Hannibal, on the Mississippi, where Samuel Clemens grew up. His pen name, Mark Twain, comes from river slang, too. Twain

Trying my
hand at the Tom Sawyer Fence Painting Contest

used Hannibal and its people in books about Tom Sawyer and Huckleberry Finn. Now his boyhood home is a museum, next to the most famous fence in American literature—the one Tom Sawyer tricked his friends into painting for him.

Nearby Marceline was where another kind of storyteller grew up—Walt Disney. More good storytellers and singers—the fiddle is the state musical instrument—can be found in the Ozarks. These are low mountains with 10,000 natural springs, and caves to explore. Missouri has more caves than any other state.

I thought Missouri should be called the Halfway State. It's halfway between the Atlantic Ocean and the Rocky Mountains, halfway between Canada and the Gulf of Mexico. But Grandma said this is the Show Me state. "Show Me" means something like "Prove It!" Missouri is spirited and stubborn. It's where the first covered wagons to California started out. Charles Lindbergh thought of here when he named his famous plane the *Spirit of St. Louis.* And Missouri even raises more mules, which are known for their stubbornness, than any other state.

WEIRD MISSOURI FACT

The most powerful earthquake in America shook up New Madrid in 1812. It was strong enough to change the course of the Mississippi River. Scientists believe another big quake will hit here before the year 2000, affecting 21 states.

Missouri mules

61

Arkansas

Looking for diamonds!

There we were, digging around in the mud . . . looking for DIAMONDS! The best time to look for diamonds is after a heavy rain, in case you want to try. Arkansas has the only diamond mine in North America—the Crater of Diamonds State Park near Murfreesboro. Anyone can hunt, and it's "finders keepers." Every day, two or three diamonds are found, not to mention amethysts, garnets, opals, and agates. You look for anything that sparkles in the sun. That sun is hot—good thing we wore hats.

We broke for lunch: hickory-smoked ham sandwiches and big juicy peaches. Grandma was reading a book called *Black Boy* by Richard Wright, all about his childhood in Arkansas.

Then "back to the mines." Too bad, no jewels for us. But we did find a piece of quartz crystal. Crystal has been used in making radios; now many people think it has healing qualities. Crystal hunters come to Arkansas from all over America. Arkansas also ranks first in several minerals.

And it has more mineral *springs* than anywhere else in America. Hot Springs, which consists of 47 springs, yields more than a million gallons of hot mineral water every day. Some people believe the mineral water can cure certain ailments.

Well, Grandma and I had fun traveling around

Hot Springs

CAPITAL: **Little Rock**

MOTTO: *Regnat Populus* (The People Rule)

We kick up our heels at the Ozark Folk Center

Guess what—Grandma's pretty good at square-dancing. I found that out at Ozark Folk Center at Mountain View. It's a state park dedicated to preserving pioneer ways of doing things, like quilt making, wood carving, playing old-timey music with dulcimers and banjos, telling stories—and square-dancing.

You know what sounds like music to me? That southern accent, smooth as peach butter. I could listen to it forever.

> **PLACES IN ARKANSAS WE WERE SORRY TO MISS**
>
> 1. Yellville, and its National Wild Turkey Calling Contest and Turkey Trot Festival. There's even a Miss Drumstick beauty contest, based on legs only.
> 2. A square mile around Rich Mountain near Mena, which has more species of wildflowers and weeds than anywhere else in the world.
> 3. Chalk Bluff, which contains enough chalk to keep my teachers at school writing happily on chalkboards for hundreds of years.
> 4. Hope, birthplace of President Bill Clinton, and where the world's biggest watermelon was grown in 1985 (try 260 pounds!).

Arkansas, listening to mountain music on the radio. That is, when we weren't singing "The Arkansas Traveler" very loudly. That's a funny conversation-song and fiddle tune that starts, "Oh, once upon a time in Arkansas . . ."

Half of Arkansas is covered with emerald green forest. The rest is made up of cotton fields, cattle ranches, bayous, and swamps—something for everybody, especially farmers. The percentage of Arkansas's population that is rural is one of the highest in America. We stopped and washed our clothes in two states at the same time: Texas and Arkansas. In a coin laundry at a place called Texarkana—what else?

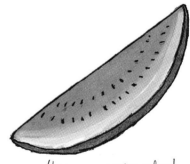

Yum . . . watermelon!

Louisiana

We *ate* our way through Louisiana—foods I've never tasted anywhere else. Grandma said it's because Louisiana has an unusual range of people. Cajuns are descended from French-speaking Acadians from Nova Scotia, and Creoles are descended from the original French and Spanish settlers.

Louisiana is full of bayous and swamps. The Spanish moss hanging from cypress trees makes me think of mysteries . . . like pirate treasure buried nearby, or the strange magic of voodoo, or ghosts haunting these old mansions. Half the ducks and geese in North America winter in Louisiana—those lucky ducks. Louisiana has 900,000 acres of wildlife preserves. One of the largest heron colonies is here, and three of the largest egret colonies.

The first thing I noticed about New Orleans was the cemeteries. More than one-third of the city's surface is water—the highest percentage of any American city. Huge pumps constantly remove water so the city doesn't disappear! With the land so watery, people are buried above ground. The clusters of marble tombs look like little cities.

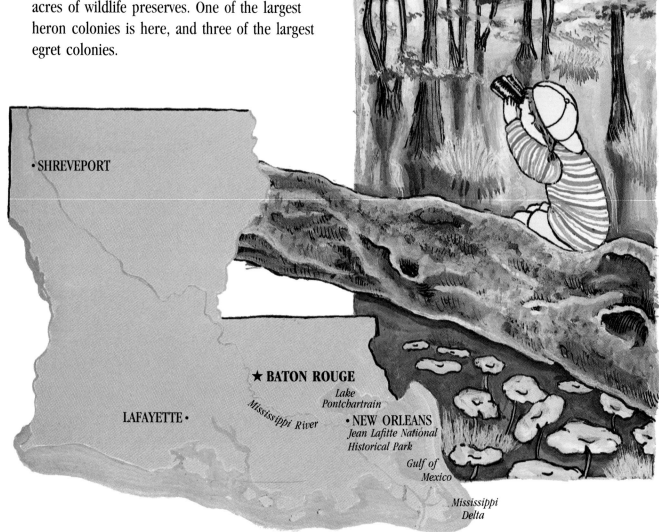

On the bayou

• SHREVEPORT

★ **BATON ROUGE**

LAFAYETTE •

Mississippi River

Lake Pontchartrain

• **NEW ORLEANS**
Jean Lafitte National Historical Park

Gulf of Mexico

Mississippi Delta

CAPITAL: **Baton Rouge**

MOTTO: **Union, Justice, and Confidence**

The French Quarter in New Orleans

New Orleans is like a dream. Now I know why some people call it America's most interesting city. We walked on cobblestone streets through the famous French Quarter and heard *all* kinds of music. Musicians like trumpeter Louis Armstrong made New Orleans famous as "the cradle of jazz." We also heard Cajun folk music (which uses fiddle, washboard, and accordion), zydeco (the African American version of Cajun music), and gospel singing. Too bad we missed Mardi Gras, America's most famous carnival. Each spring, New Orleans goes wild with parties.

An interesting place near here is Jean Lafitte National Historical Park, site of the Battle of New Orleans. Andrew Jackson's troops were joined by America's best-known pirates, Jean and Pierre Lafitte, and they beat the British during the War of 1812.

FABULOUS FOODS IN LOUISIANA

1. Blackened redfish: fish served black with lots of spices.
2. Gumbo, bisque, and bouillabaisse: spicy seafood soups. With enough pepper to make my mouth water—sometimes my eyes, too!
3. Jambalaya: a sticky rice with shrimp, sausage, and chicken.
4. Frog legs: Louisiana has more frogs than any other state!
5. Shrimp creole: Louisiana is first in shrimp, too.
6. Cajun popcorn: fresh crawfish boiled in spicy oil.
7. Huge sandwiches called *muffulettas* and po'boys.
8. Oysters: New Orleans has at least 50 oyster bars.
9. *Beignets,* or hot, puffy doughnuts piled with powdered sugar.
10. King cake, decorated in Mardi Gras colors, with a trinket baked inside. The person who bites into the trinket, usually a plastic baby, has to buy the next king cake.

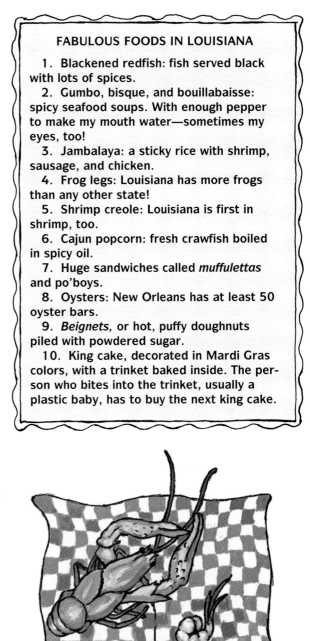

Louisiana seafood

Mississippi

"M-I-S-S-I-S-S-I-P-P-I . . ."

Grandma and I sang and spelled as we rolled into the state named after the world's largest river. The Mississippi River might look like a bunch of brown water—I can see why it's called Big Muddy—but it's important water. It's a liquid highway that borders ten states, including Mississippi, of course. It passes through much of America, brings things from one place to another, and makes people think about our history. When the river gets *too* important, it floods and causes great damage. Levees, or artificial riverbanks, hold the water back and keep houses from being washed away.

We stopped for a piece of Mississippi mud pie—delicious: it's chocolate, not mud. We enjoyed the warm, sunny day, with its pink and purple azaleas, sweet-smelling magnolia trees, and loblollies as white as wax.

Mississippi is musical, even in the names of rivers and towns. At one place along the Pascagoula River, we heard the water "singing." This is the mysterious Singing River, famous for buzzing during evening stillness. No one knows what makes the sound.

Mississippi is a rural state, with more tree farms than any other state. Most people live on farms. The Mississippi-Yazoo Delta, created by the Mississippi River, has some of the richest soil in the world. It has some rich people, too—and also some poor people. Grandma said this is where you can see the biggest contrast in America between the lives of the very rich, like the plantation owners, and the very poor, like the workers.

Playing the blues on the banks of Big Muddy

CAPITAL: **Jackson**

MOTTO: *Virtute et Armis* **(By Valor and Arms)**

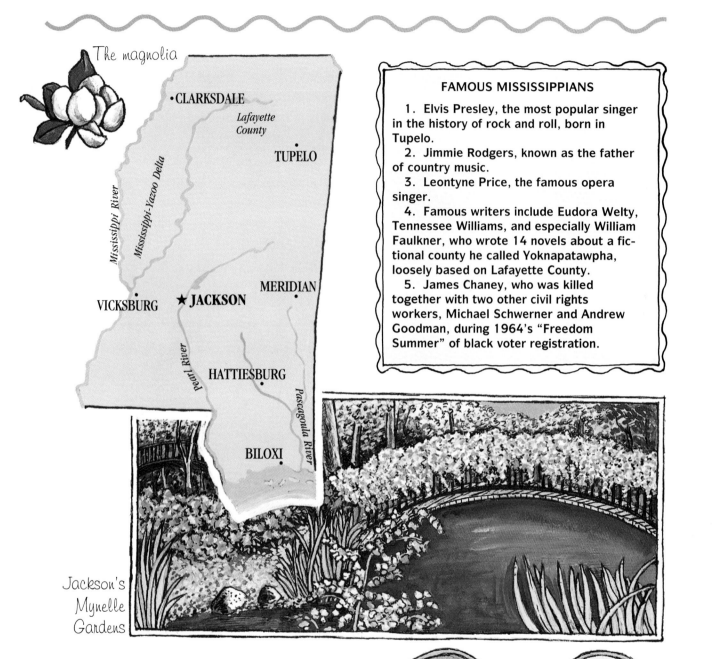

The magnolia

CLARKSDALE

Lafayette County

TUPELO

Mississippi River

Mississippi-Yazoo Delta

MERIDIAN

VICKSBURG ★ JACKSON

Pearl River

HATTIESBURG

Pascagoula River

BILOXI

Jackson's Mynelle Gardens

FAMOUS MISSISSIPPIANS

1. Elvis Presley, the most popular singer in the history of rock and roll, born in Tupelo.
2. Jimmie Rodgers, known as the father of country music.
3. Leontyne Price, the famous opera singer.
4. Famous writers include Eudora Welty, Tennessee Williams, and especially William Faulkner, who wrote 14 novels about a fictional county he called Yoknapatawpha, loosely based on Lafayette County.
5. James Chaney, who was killed together with two other civil rights workers, Michael Schwerner and Andrew Goodman, during 1964's "Freedom Summer" of black voter registration.

Mississippi has the highest percentage of African Americans of any state—and more black elected officials than any other state. In Clarksdale, we visited the Delta Blues Museum, dedicated to preserving the history of the Mississippi Delta blues. We heard recordings of W. C. Handy and John Lee Hooker playing the music that was eventually popular all over the world.

Richard Wright

Eudora Welty

Tennessee

Is Elvis alive? Some people think so! Elvis Presley's *music* is alive, but the "King" was buried in 1977, in the garden at Graceland, the mansion named after his mother. Thousands tour here each day. We saw his trophies and cars and his private jet named the *Lisa Marie,* for his daughter.

The place to come if you want to be a star is Nashville. It's just as musical as Memphis—it's the country music capital of America. Next to Las Vegas, Nashville has more entertainers per person than any other city.

The world's largest broadcasting studio is here, and also Opryland, U.S.A., the only musical amusement park in America. My favorite part of Tennessee was the show we saw at the Grand Ole Opry House. I've never been to a music show where the audience went so wild.

Tennessee is supermusical. Besides Graceland, Memphis has one of the most famous streets in America: Beale Street, considered the blues capital of the South. People like B. B. King started out here, playing the blues, what some consider America's first truly original music. Memphis also has the National Civil Rights Museum, where we learned about milestones in the modern civil rights movement.

Tennessee has not one but *two* state songs: "Rocky Top" and "Tennessee Waltz." Even the trains here are musical. Chattanooga, an important railroad town, was made famous in the "Chattanooga Choo-Choo" song.

CAPITAL: **Nashville**

MOTTO: **Agriculture and Commerce**

Too bad we missed the National Storytelling Festival, held every October in Jonesboro. On the last night of it, everyone goes to the cemetery and listens to ghost stories.

Half of Tennessee is forest. In fact, the most famous Tennessee image is of lonely pioneers wearing coonskin caps, blazing a path through the forest. Maybe they were carrying guitars, too—singing a song as they explored!

Great Smoky Mountains National Park

In the Great Smoky Mountains National Park, shared with North Carolina, there are other kinds of music: babbling waterfalls and the breeze ruffling through leafy trees. For a long time, this area was so remote that people still spoke Elizabethan English. Now this is the most visited national park in America. We stopped for a special southern meal of grits (bleached corn ground into coarse dry form), hush puppies (little cornmeal dumplings), turnip greens, biscuits, and apple cobbler.

FAMOUS TENNESSEANS

1. Davy Crockett was the subject of legends, but also a real Tennessee politician and hunter. His motto was "Be always sure you're right, then go ahead."

2. Charles Saunders established America's first supermarkets, in Memphis in 1916. He called them Piggly-Wiggly . . . after a game he saw his children playing with their toes.

3. The first guide dog for the blind in America was Buddy, a German shepherd in Nashville, trained in 1928.

Davy Crockett's birthplace

Alabama

Picking cotton

(they're flowers!) back to all the Susans I know at school. Grandma loved seeing the well-preserved antebellum mansions, which are huge houses built before the Civil War.

There are lots of historic places in Alabama. Montgomery is said to be the birthplace of the civil rights movement against racial discrimination; Dr. Martin Luther King, Jr., began his career at the Dexter Avenue King Memorial Baptist Church here. Tuscumbia is where Helen Keller, the blind and deaf humanitarian, was born. Hank Aaron, the great baseball player, was born in Mobile. Florence is where W. C. Handy, known as the father of the blues, was born. In Tuskegee,

I have to say I've never seen snow in the summer before. But that's just what the cotton fields here look like. Alabama used to be "snowy" all over. Then bugs called boll weevils started eating the cotton. Farmers had to grow soybeans and corn and peanuts instead of depending on just one crop.

There's something else snowy white in Alabama: the sand at Gulf Shores, on the Gulf of Mexico, 50 miles of some of the prettiest beaches in America. There are warm air, warm waters, and warm southern hospitality. The sand is the color and texture of sugar. It *squeaked* when I walked on it! The blue-green waves are so clear you can see schools of colorful creatures: blue crabs and red snapper and black bass. We waited for low tide and collected shells for souvenirs.

Nearby Mobile is a beautiful city. I wish I could take a bunch of these black-eyed Susans

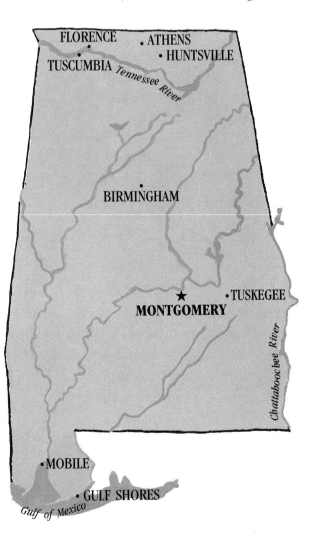

CAPITAL: **Montgomery**

MOTTO: *Audemus Jura Nostra Defendere*
(We Dare Defend Our Rights)

Grandma in the Man Maneuvering Unit,
U.S. Space and Rocket Center

to make rockets to take people to the moon. The best part of all was more than 60 hands-on exhibits that let me become an astronaut for a day. I felt all the sights, sounds, tastes, and gravity force of a flight to the moon. "3 . . . 2 . . . 1 . . . Blast-off!"

FAMOUS ALABAMA QUOTATION

"Damn the torpedoes! Full speed ahead!"
—said by Admiral David Farragut during the Civil War as he ran ships through Mobile Bay

---

MUSICAL MOMENTS IN ALABAMA

In October, there's the Tennessee Valley Old-Time Fiddlers' Convention in the hill country of Athens. It draws thousands of visitors, and hundreds of musicians who play fiddle, banjo, and dulcimer. "Oh, Susanna," "Down in the Valley," "Follow the Drinking Gourd," and "The Mockingbird Song (Hush, Little Baby)" are all folk songs with Alabama connections.

---

there are museums in honor of George Washington Carver, the agricultural chemist whose research helped Alabama branch out from cotton; and Booker T. Washington, the famous educator.

You can see the past *and* the future in Alabama. In Huntsville we blasted off at the U.S. Space and Rocket Center, Earth's largest space museum. This is where America figured out how

Marching for civil rights, 1965

Florida

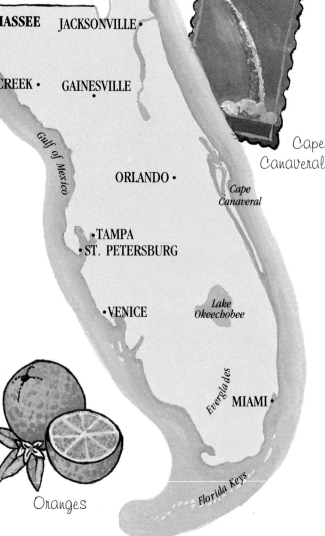

★ **TALLAHASSEE** JACKSONVILLE •

CROSS CREEK • GAINESVILLE •

Gulf of Mexico

ORLANDO •

Cape Canaveral

Cape Canaveral

• TAMPA
• ST. PETERSBURG

Lake Okeechobee

• VENICE

Everglades

MIAMI •

Florida Keys

Oranges

Florida makes me think of orange and pink: The bag of **oranges** I bought as a souvenir. (Florida supplies two-thirds of America's oranges, and orange juice is the state drink.) Fiery **orange** sunsets. (The sun is more powerful in this southernmost of the lower 48 states; Florida looks like a big toe stretching toward the equator.) The **orange** and **pink** buildings of the Art Deco District in Miami. (Know why Miami is sometimes called the capital of Latin America? Because Hispanics are more than 50 percent of the countywide population.) **Pink** flamingos. **Orange** and **pink** flowers. **Pink** papayas we ate with sugar. (Half of all sugar in America comes from here.) And my new **pink** bathing suit. (Florida is nearly surrounded by water, with 1,800 miles of

beaches and more lakes than any other state.)

Early explorers were looking for a Fountain of Youth. Now people dream of retiring here. One out of five Floridians is a senior citizen, and the state song is Stephen Foster's "Old Folks at Home." With its coconut palm trees swaying in the breeze, Florida is just the place to get warm. It's said that 800 people move here each day, and Floridians have more houseguests than any

The Carlyle

Groovin' in Miami

other state. Spring brings mobs of college students on their breaks and baseball teams for spring practice. Venice is the winter home of the Ringling Brothers and Barnum & Bailey Circus, which tries out its new routines here.

Walt Disney World at Orlando is the world's largest amusement park. I liked Future World the best, at EPCOT Center, which stands for Experimental Prototype Community Of Tomorrow. Nearby Cape Canaveral is the launching pad for America's ventures into outer space. That makes it one of the most famous spots on Earth.

We took a muggy canoe ride through the Everglades—more than one million acres of some of the rarest plants and animals in America. This is also home to the Seminole people still remaining in Florida. Paddling underneath a canopy of dense foliage, we felt as if we were going back in time. Grandma was reading *The Yearling* by Marjorie Kinnan Rawlings, who lived in Cross Creek, a backwoods town near Gainesville.

The Florida Keys are a mellow strip of islands connected by 42 bridges. We rode in a glass-bottom boat off Key Largo for a close-up look at America's first underwater park. You can see 55 types of coral, hundreds of species of tropical fish and sea creatures, and the remains of ships wrecked on the reefs. The tip of Florida, Key West, is only 90 miles from Cuba. It was originally home to the pirates of the Caribbean. Some restaurants here serve alligator meat, but we just had a snack: big pieces of key lime pie— a tart sort of pudding-pie made from key limes.

**FLORIDA KEYS
TO INTERESTING MYSTERIES**

Why can you hear the ocean when you put a pink conch shell next to your ear? (It's really the sound of air going through the shell.) Why does Florida have the highest rate of deaths from lightning? (Because it has more lightning than any other state.)

Snorkeling in the Florida Keys

Georgia

The next day we were "gone with the wind" . . . to Atlanta, Georgia.

Grandma says that Georgia's most famous writer is Margaret Mitchell, who wrote *Gone with the Wind* at the Atlanta Public Library. At a Civil War exhibit in Grant Park, we saw an enormous painting of the movie's most famous scene: the Burning of Atlanta, in which most of the city was destroyed. It's hard not to notice the history of the Civil War all around Georgia. One interesting place was the Blue and Gray Museum in Fitzgerald. It has artifacts from both the Union (blue) and Confederate (gray) sides of the war.

They did a good job of rebuilding Atlanta! Now it's the "city too busy to hate"—a pretty, glittering place said to be the most densely wooded city in America. In spring, it's a fairyland, with flowering trees of all kinds.

Another famous writer who lived here was Joel Chandler Harris. He wrote his Uncle Remus stories about Brer Rabbit in a house called The Wren's Nest. Besides trees and writers, Atlanta is famous for Coca-Cola. It was invented in a drugstore here in 1886, originally made from *coca* leaves and *cola* nuts.

Be prepared! Savannah was the birthplace of the Girl Scouts and its founder, Juliette Gordon Low. Savannah also has the largest National Historic Landmark District in America. That means

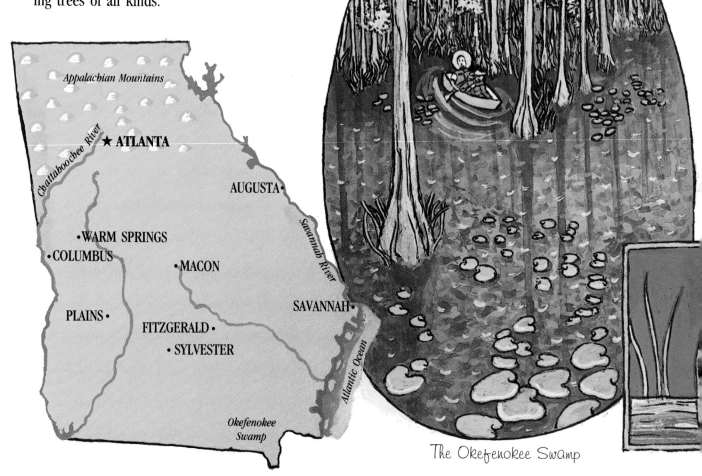

The Okefenokee Swamp

74

CAPITAL: **Atlanta**

MOTTO: **Wisdom, Justice, and Moderation**

Fancy living in Savannah

it's full of gorgeous old mansions shaded by more of those leafy trees. We wished we were sitting on one of those old verandas, drinking lemonade and playing the harmonica.

Forests cover most of Georgia. The expression "tall as a Georgia pine" comes from here. Surprise! There are hills and mountains to the north, red clay country in the middle, and a hundred miles of coastline to the southeast.

We rented a boat and explored a kind of spooky place: the Okefenokee Swamp, one of the last natural swamp areas in the country. Seminoles called it "the land of the trembling earth." It's a collection of floating islands so shaky that many have never been explored. It's also home to the largest alligators in North America. Eeeks!

For dinner we had fried chicken (Georgia leads all states in poultry production) and baked squash. I had peach cobbler for dessert, and Grandma had pecan pie. The next day we tried boiled peanuts, which are peanuts boiled in the shell till smooth. Everyone knows that Georgia is first in peanut farming. In fact, the biggest peanut in the world was grown here, in Sylvester in 1987.

The birthplace of Martin Luther King, Jr.

VERY IMPORTANT GEORGIANS

1. Atlanta was the birthplace of Dr. Martin Luther King, Jr., the man most responsible for civil rights legislation outlawing racial discrimination. The Martin Luther King, Jr., Center for Nonviolent Change is in downtown Atlanta.

2. Jimmy Carter, from Plains, was in 1976 the first Georgian to be elected U.S. president.

3. President Franklin D. Roosevelt had a home in Warm Springs and died there in 1945. His friendships here influenced his presidential policies.

An American alligator

South Carolina

A Charleston mansion

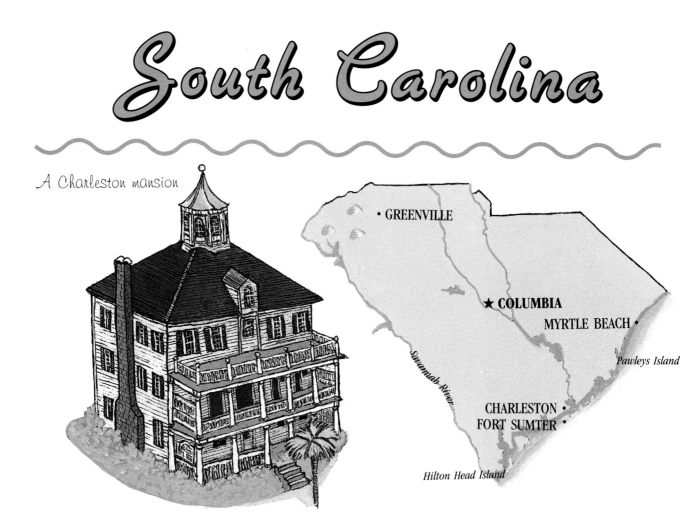

- • GREENVILLE
- ★ COLUMBIA
- MYRTLE BEACH •
- *Pawleys Island*
- *Savannah River*
- CHARLESTON •
- FORT SUMTER •
- *Hilton Head Island*

King Charles I of England must have been some king—to get *two* American states named after him. One is South and one is North: the Carolinas. South Carolina is full of palmetto trees and colors: pale pink and snowy white azaleas, lavender wisteria, yellow Carolina jessamine, red-purple rhododendrons.

When we hit Charleston, Grandma got out of the car and did a wild dance for me. She said it was the Charleston, the most popular dance of the 1920's—named after this gorgeous city. This place has hundreds of carefully preserved pastel mansions hundreds of years old. They have porches, called piazzas, on narrow brick alleys, and formal gardens. People actually live in these old, old houses, but they're famous for hospitality and are nice enough to open them up sometimes for visitors to have a peek. We stopped for a snack of peaches, the state fruit, and milk, the state beverage.

Charleston had the first museum and the first theater in America, and also the first opera and the first symphony orchestra. America's first woman artist lived here—Henrietta Johnson, a portrait painter who started out in 1707. Across the water, the first shots of the Civil War were fired at Fort Sumter, in 1861. South Carolina was the first state to secede from the Union, which is how the Civil War started.

Grandma among the palmettos

CAPITAL: **Columbia**

MOTTO: *Dum Spiro Spero* **(While I Breathe, I Hope);**
Animus Opibusque Parati **(Prepared in Mind
and Resources)**

Trying out a Pawleys Island hammock

Grandma told me how Charleston blacks living on Cabbage Row inspired DuBose Heyward and George Gershwin's "Catfish Row," in the American opera *Porgy and Bess.* Another musical fact: Black tobacco workers in Charleston picked "We Shall Overcome," an old hymn, as their theme song in 1946. This went on to become the best-known protest song of the 1960's.

South Carolina has a long coastline. It is called the Grand Strand of sand. Myrtle Beach is the most popular destination for vacationers on the East Coast, after Walt Disney World in Florida and Atlantic City in New Jersey. We built a giant sand castle in Myrtle Beach, in honor of one of the longest sand sculptures ever built. The Never-Ending Fantasy once took up nearly three miles of Myrtle Beach!

Time for a rest. What better place than nearby Pawleys Island, famous for its handmade hammocks? It's also famous for ghosts. Huge haunted houses here have doors that creak and shutters that bang. The "Gray Man" ghost is said to appear just before a hurricane. Boo!

**SOME THINGS NORTH AND SOUTH
CAROLINA HAVE IN COMMON**

1. Sunken treasure. Hundreds of ships have sunk on treacherous Carolina shores. Some were carrying millions of dollars in gold when they sank.

2. Buried treasure. Both coasts are probably the best places in America to dig. Pirates like Blackbeard used these lonely beaches as hiding grounds.

3. Clothes. If you're wearing American clothes, chances are about one in four they were made in North or South Carolina.

4. Last but not least: the Venus's-flytrap. These are the only two states where this insect-trapping plant grows wild!

Diving for treasure!

North Carolina

There's something about Kitty Hawk that made me feel like flying.

And I'm not the only one. The world's first successful airplane flight took place here in 1903. Wilbur and Orville Wright's first flight lasted 12 seconds, but they got better later. Kitty Hawk is isolated and has steady breezes, tall dunes, and endless sand: the perfect place to launch a plane—or a trip through North Carolina.

We were on the Outer Banks, the islands that protect the North Carolina shore from stormy waters. On a calm day it's hard to tell where the blue sea ends and the blue sky begins. One thing sticking out is the Cape Hatteras Lighthouse, Amer-ica's tallest lighthouse. Grandma said people need a good lighthouse here, on the stormiest coastline of the Atlantic Ocean. So many ships sink here that Cape Hatteras is known as the graveyard of the Atlantic.

Inland, near Chapel Hill, we cooled off by diving into an old-fashioned swimming hole, the kind I've seen pictures of in books. We floated on our backs and looked up at the amazingly tall trees. You could be sitting on a piece of North Carolina right now. Grandma said that much of America's wood furniture comes from here. Some of the trees had kudzu, a vine that creeps all over everything in its way. My favorite trees were the

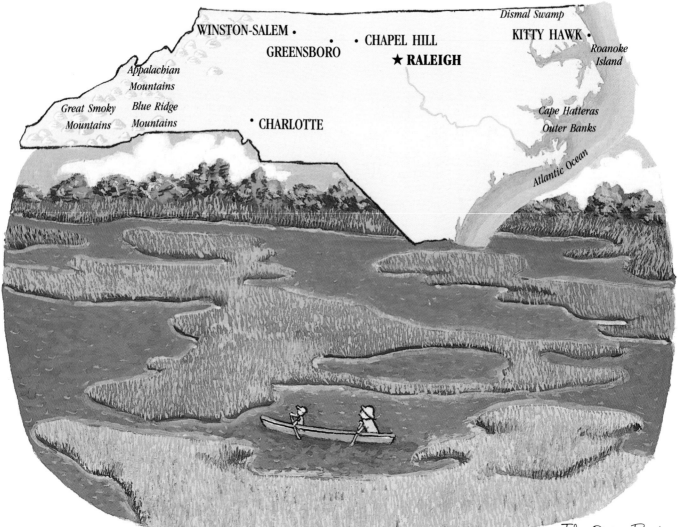

WINSTON-SALEM •
• CHAPEL HILL
GREENSBORO •
★ RALEIGH
KITTY HAWK •
Dismal Swamp
Roanoke Island
Appalachian Mountains
Great Smoky Mountains
Blue Ridge Mountains
• CHARLOTTE
Cape Hatteras
Outer Banks
Atlantic Ocean

The Outer Banks

The Great Smoky Mountains

graceful weeping willows. For dinner we had North Carolina's specialty, barbecued pork, with crunchy coleslaw and sweet potato pie. This state is first in sweet potatoes.

North Carolina is humid. Watch out for giant cockroaches. But it's never too hot or too cold. It's protected by some very famous mountains. On a drive through the Blue Ridge Mountains, part of the Appalachians shared with Virginia, we saw hills overgrown by wild summer roses. The Great Smoky Mountains, shared with Tennessee and also part of the Appalachians, are some of the oldest mountains in North America. You know the song "On Top of Old Smoky"? It's in honor of the smoky blue haze of these giant old hills.

The first settlers on these beautiful hills were Cherokee people, led for a long time by Chief Sequoyah. Grandma told me that in the 1830's the American government decided to drive the Cherokee away. More than one-fourth of them died on the Trail of Tears on their way to Oklahoma. But some remained behind, and today, North Carolina has the largest number of American Indians of any state east of the Mississippi River.

WEIRD NORTH CAROLINA FACTS

1. Virginia Dare was the first baby born in the first English colony in North America, on Roanoke Island in 1587. The weird part: Months later, the whole colony (including Virginia) disappeared without a trace . . . except for the single word "Croatoan," the name of a local American Indian people, carved on a tree. No one has ever found out what happened to this Lost Colony.

2. This is the leading tobacco state. The weird part: More than a third of first-grade boys in rural North Carolina have tried chewing tobacco.

At the ole swimming hole

Virginia

I always wondered what it was like to live in Colonial America, back in the 1700's. Then Grandma took me to Williamsburg—America's most important restored Colonial village—and I found out. All the buildings here look just the same as in the days when Virginia was *the* place to live. My favorite part was the craft workshops. We saw blacksmiths pounding on glowing iron, cabinetmakers carving chairs, and wigmakers, weavers, glassblowers, and bookbinders. We even visited the jail, which used to hold pirates. At lunch, a waiter dressed in Colonial clothes brought us Virginia ham sandwiches. I wonder if Thomas Jefferson, George Washington, and Patrick Henry used to meet in this very restaurant.

A few miles away is Carter's Grove plantation on the James River. Robert Carter was probably America's first millionaire. His mansion has been called the most beautiful house in America, and I can see why. The stairway is simply spectacular. But the railing has deep scars in it, said to have been made by an angry British soldier riding his horse up the stairs!

Grandma said Virginia is alive with history. Jamestown Island, for example, is the site of the first permanent English settlement in America. Here is where Pocahontas, the Powhatan Indian princess, is said to have saved the life of Captain John Smith. She also taught the English how to grow tobacco, which became Virginia's main crop. Mount Vernon was George Washington's home, conveniently close to his job in Washington, D.C. Monticello is where Thomas Jefferson lived. Besides being president, Jefferson was once ambassador to France—and he served the first french fries in America, here at Monticello.

Colonial Williamsburg

ARLINGTON
WASHINGTON, D.C.
Mount Vernon

Potomac River

Atlantic Ocean

Monticello

Appalachian Mountains

Blue Ridge Mountains

James River

★ **RICHMOND**

Delmarva Peninsula

WILLIAMSBURG •

Jamestown Island

Chesapeake Bay

• **ROANOKE**

NORFOLK •

VIRGINIA BEACH •

Dismal Swamp

Cumberland Gap

CAPITAL: **Richmond**
MOTTO: *Sic Semper Tyrannis* (Thus Always to Tyrants)

Helping guard the Jamestown Settlement

You always hear about the Pentagon, the American military headquarters. Well, we saw it—the world's largest office building, with the world's largest parking lot. It has 280 bathrooms alone! The whole thing is in the shape of a pentagon—you know, with five sides.

Virginia also has the largest pleasure beach in the world: Virginia Beach, 38 miles on the Atlantic Ocean. No wonder people in Norfolk–Virginia Beach buy more boating magazines than do Americans in any other area.

Virginia Beach

Virginia has the most famous cemetery in the country: Arlington National Cemetery, just across from the Lincoln Memorial. Americans who served their country are buried here, including Ludwig Bemelmans (who wrote the Madeline books); Abner Doubleday (the founder of baseball); John F. Kennedy and Robert F. Kennedy; and astronauts who died in accidents. The Tomb of the Unknowns honors those Americans killed in war who could not be identified.

VIRGINIA AS A MOM AND DAD

Four out of five of the first American presidents were from Virginia (George Washington, Thomas Jefferson, James Madison, and James Monroe). In all, eight presidents were born here. No wonder it's called the "Mother" of presidents. And the "Father" of states: Eight other states were formed from land that used to be part of Virginia—West Virginia, for example.

Arlington National Cemetery

West Virginia

Whoosh! This was the wildest adventure of all: whitewater rafting down West Virginia's New River. Gliding through narrow canyons, Grandma and I held on to our paddles for dear life. Our guide called this part of the river a good trip for beginners—whew! I'd hate to raft down the sections for experts! Water splashed in our faces, while the warm breeze worked to keep us dry. This was the most fun I've ever had while being scared at the same time.

West Virginia is called the whitewater capital of the East, with about nine rivers suitable for rafting. The New River, which is actually America's *oldest* river, cuts through the entire state. The New River Gorge is called the Grand Canyon of the East. Places like Berkeley Springs and White Sulphur Springs are considered some of the finest resorts in America. I guess there's hardly a town here without a river, lake, or creek. This state has some of America's most rugged terrain, zooming up and down without much level ground. No wonder it's called America's Little Switzerland.

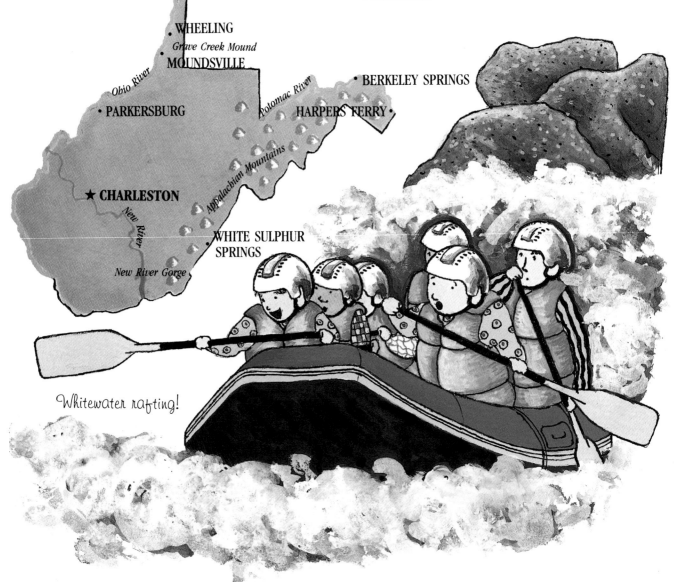

WHEELING
Grave Creek Mound
MOUNDSVILLE
Ohio River
• PARKERSBURG
Potomac River
• BERKELEY SPRINGS
HARPERS FERRY
Appalachian Mountains
★ CHARLESTON
New River
WHITE SULPHUR SPRINGS
New River Gorge

Whitewater rafting!

CAPITAL: **Charleston**

MOTTO: *Montani Semper Liberi*
(Mountaineers Are Always Free)

If you live in West Virginia, it helps to be a mountaineer—the independent type. West Virginia is *such* an independent place that it broke away from its parent, Virginia, when the Civil War started, because it wanted to fight on the other side. We saw Harpers Ferry, a pretty town made famous by John Brown's raid, one of the causes of the Civil War in the first place.

West Virginia was a favorite hunting ground for many American Indian nations and groups. The first people to live here were the prehistoric Mound Builders. We toured the Grave Creek Mound at Moundsville. It's the largest prehistoric burial mound of its kind in the world. Built from many tons of earth, it contains burial chambers, tools and ornaments, and tablets of writing. Very mysterious: Even now, no one knows just why the Mound Builders went to all this trouble to bury people.

West Virginia is most famous for coal, with lots of coal mines underneath these mountains. This

Grandma tries out glassblowing

state makes glass, too. In fact, most of America's glass marbles come from factories in Parkersburg.

Southern Appalachian culture is important here, with mountain crafts festivals all over, and the sounds of dulcimers and banjos. West Virginia is such a musical place that it has not one, not two, but three state songs.

Cabin Creek, a coal town

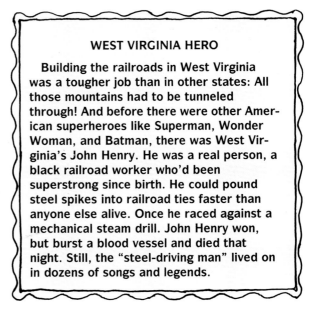

WEST VIRGINIA HERO

Building the railroads in West Virginia was a tougher job than in other states: All those mountains had to be tunneled through! And before there were other American superheroes like Superman, Wonder Woman, and Batman, there was West Virginia's John Henry. He was a real person, a black railroad worker who'd been superstrong since birth. He could pound steel spikes into railroad ties faster than anyone else alive. Once he raced against a mechanical steam drill. John Henry won, but burst a blood vessel and died that night. Still, the "steel-driving man" lived on in dozens of songs and legends.

District of Columbia

The Lincoln Memorial

The U.S. Capitol

Is the District of Columbia a state, a city, or what? Well, it's 69 square miles along the Potomac River. They were donated by Maryland to be set aside as a district. The "Columbia" part comes from good old Christopher COLUMBUS. The city of Washington covers the entire District of Columbia. Now, just as each state has its own capital, Washington—named after George, of course—is the capital of the whole United States.

Washington is a city of V.I.B.'s: Very Important Buildings. The one at 1600 Pennsylvania Avenue, for example, is the White House. The President and First Lady live in just a few of its 132 rooms. I liked Jacqueline Kennedy's famous Rose Garden. Grandma liked the East Room, where the President holds press conferences. There are more news reporters in Washington than anywhere else—and more newspaper *readers* per person, by far. Wouldn't it be super to be president someday? I could live here with my First Man.

The Capitol is a round building where our 100 senators (two from each state) and 435 representatives go to work. The Senate and the House of Representatives together make up the Congress—the important people who make our laws. No building taller that 13 stories is allowed in Washington. That way, the dome of the Capitol can always be seen above the city. We had breakfast at the Capitol Coffee Shop and looked for famous politicians.

The Supreme Court building has 16 columns of white marble. This is where the nine most important judges in America make decisions about how the U.S. Constitution applies to new situations.

The Washington Monument looks like a giant pencil. We took the elevator up (70 seconds) . . . then huffed and puffed down the 898 steps. But seeing the spectacular view of the city was worth it. The Lincoln Memorial has a 19-foot-high statue of Lincoln. Martin Luther King, Jr., gave his famous "I have a dream" speech on the steps here in 1963. Another emotional place is the Vietnam Veterans Memorial—black marble walls inscribed with the names of all 58,132 Americans who died in the Vietnam War. This is now the most visited site in Washington.

The Smithsonian Institution is the world's largest museum complex. My favorite was the National Gallery of Art. Wow! Grandma loved the Library of Congress, the largest library in the world—try 97 million items, or 10 new items a minute! This is where the Library of Congress Cataloging-in-Publication data, like what you see at the beginning of *this* book, comes from.

Many of these buildings are around a huge park called the Mall. Now when I hear about people going to Washington for demonstrations, I'll know this is where everyone gathers.

Government is the main business in Washing-

At the Library of Congress

ton. Most workers live in Maryland or Virginia. Seventy percent of the residents are African American, the largest percentage of any American city, and many of them live in poverty. Many people favor making D.C. our 51st state, so it would have its own voting representatives in Congress. It would be called New Columbia.

The list of things to see and do here is just endless. As a city, state, district, or whatever . . . Washington is worth many trips.

The Vietnam
Veterans Memorial

Maryland

Somewhere deep in Maryland, I saw why it's called America in miniature.

This state has many things found all over: busy cities, colorful towns, sandy beaches, rocky mountains and cliffs, rich farmland and fabulous fishing, pine forests, marshy lowlands, many ethnic groups (and their foods), and people, some very rich and some very poor. And a lot of history: Annapolis has the highest concentration of eighteenth-century buildings in America.

But Maryland is small—a miniature America—and it has the weirdest shape. It's cut almost in two by the Chesapeake Bay, and in some places is less than two miles wide. If all the curves in the bay were ironed out, the true length of Maryland's shore would be 8,000 miles.

The most mysterious place in Maryland is Assateague Island. Hundreds of years ago, a Spanish ship crashed into the coast there and sank. Somehow the ponies on board survived, and today their great-great-grandchildren live on the island, wild and free. Storms have destroyed almost all the houses on the island. Now it's a state park and a national seashore. When Grandma and I hiked a nature trail, we were able to feed two of the ponies! They find most of their food in saltwater marshes. In summer the ponies swim from Assateague to Chincoteague Island, off

Making friends on Assateague Island

Potomac River
BALTIMORE · Fort McHenry
ANNAPOLIS ★
Chesapeake Bay
Atlantic Ocean
OCEAN CITY ·
Assateague Island
Chincoteague Island

The B&O Atlantic, 1832

Delmarva Peninsula in Virginia. The water of the Chincoteague Bay churns with wild ponies! Grandma said these horses were made famous by Marguerite Henry, who wrote *Misty of Chincoteague* and other wonderful horse books.

Most people in Maryland live near Baltimore, which sort of hooks up with Washington, D.C., to make a long district of people who work for the government. And doctors, too—Maryland has more of them per person than any other state.

Baltimore has hundreds of neighborhoods, like Little Italy and Little Lithuania, with their own histories and cultures. Grandma said this was the first city in America where a person could buy a run-down house for a dollar and fix it up. Famous Baltimoreans include Edgar Allan Poe, who's buried here; baseball great Babe Ruth, who was born here; John Waters, who makes weird movies; and journalist H. L. Mencken.

We visited the B&O (which stands for Baltimore & Ohio) Railroad Museum. Before cars, before planes, and before motorcycles, trains were really important to life in America. The B&O was America's very first railroad, and its first tracks were right here.

We relaxed on a harbor cruise around Baltimore, smelling spices and sugar from nearby factories that make those very items. That made us hungry for Maryland's most famous food: crabs.

No, not crabby people, but tasty crustaceans. The Chesapeake Bay is world-famous for crabs. For generations, crabbers have caught and sold them to be eaten the same night at crab houses. Did you know that lady crabs are called sooks, and man crabs are jimmies?

Row houses in Baltimore

Delaware

WILMINGTON
Delaware River
Delaware Bay
★ DOVER
Cape Henlopen State Park
REHOBOTH BEACH •

A ship in Delaware Bay

The Old State House in Dover, built 1792

Delaware had a strange beginning. Henry Hudson discovered it while searching for a trade route to East Asia in 1609. He hoped Delaware Bay was it. It wasn't. Then it was named after someone—Thomas West, Baron De La Warr, the governor of Virginia—who was never even in Delaware.

Now it's our second-smallest state, with the fourth-fewest people. It's nine miles wide at its narrowest, and a hundred miles long altogether: only half the size of Los Angeles County.

We saw pretty farms with stone walls and old red barns. And historic old towns with quiet, tree-lined streets, sometimes paved in cobblestone. Half of Delaware is farmland. Chicken farms are to the south. Sussex County produces more broiler chickens than any other American county. Rolling hills are in the north, with thickets of cranberries and blueberries.

Stopping for lunch, we had chicken (what else?) and dumplings, and we tried scrapple—a mixture of pork and cornmeal. Grandma made us go antiques shopping. She went wild over spinning wheels and other examples of Early American this and that. I bought a tiny cameo pin as a souvenir.

My favorite spot was the Great Walking Dune of Cape Henlopen State Park. Guess what: It "walks" a few feet every year! The northwest winds along Delaware's Atlantic coast cause the sands to shift, which over time makes the dune "travel." Swashbuckling stories of the Delaware coast involved this dune.

Two-thirds of Delawareans live in and around

Wilmington. Many companies are here, since businesses like Delaware's laws. The largest company is the one owned by the du Pont family. The du Pont company invented rubber, cellophane, Teflon, and nylon, among other things. Wilmington is called the chemical capital of the world because so many chemicals are made here. And there's a lot of du Ponts, too— some 400 in Delaware, some 2,000 in all.

In Wilmington, the Hagley Museum on the Brandywine River is an outdoor history museum where we pretended we were living in the past. It has 25 homes and mills fixed up to look the way they did in the nineteenth century.

Rehoboth Beach is the best spot in Delaware for beach fun. Many workers from the Washington, D.C., area come here for vacation. And I found out that the largest flea market is in Laurel, which is also full of country auctions.

I didn't tell Grandma; I was afraid we'd never get out of Delaware.

At Rehoboth Beach

Du Pont family château at Nemours

DELAWARE FIRSTS

1. Delaware was the first of the original 13 states to sign the Constitution. That's why every four years Delaware gets to lead the parade of states at the American presidential inauguration.

2. In Delaware, Swedish immigrants built the first log cabins in America, in 1638.

3. The first of the many beauty pageants in America was at Rehoboth Beach in 1880. One of the judges back then was Thomas Edison, the inventor.

New Jersey

Today we walked up and down the Boardwalk. We strolled around Marvin Gardens and Park Place, ambled over to Ventnor Avenue and St. Charles Place, and took a look at Oriental Avenue and St. James Place. Were we trapped in a life-size game of Monopoly? Or were we in a world-famous resort town, the gambling playground of the East, the first large town devoted to parties?

Right. We were in Atlantic City, New Jersey. While we strolled, we sang "'Here she comes . . .'" —the theme song of the Miss America pageant held each September here. We ate saltwater taffy and bought picture postcards to send home. Both were invented here. And the people who invented Monopoly named its spaces after the streets in Atlantic City.

New Jersey has 127 miles of white sandy beaches and lots more resorts besides Atlantic City. When we stopped at a roadside stand and bought tomatoes, we found out that New Jersey's

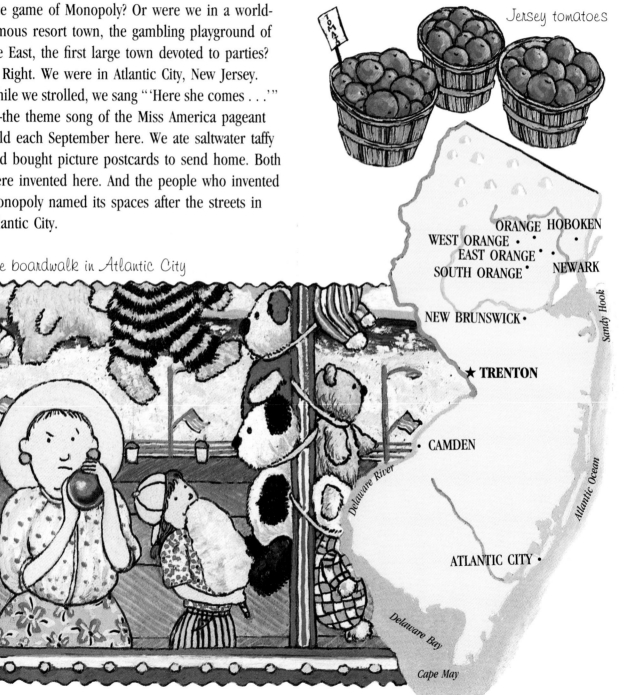

Jersey tomatoes

On the boardwalk in Atlantic City

ORANGE HOBOKEN
WEST ORANGE
EAST ORANGE
SOUTH ORANGE   NEWARK

NEW BRUNSWICK

★ TRENTON

CAMDEN

Sandy Hook

Delaware River

Atlantic Ocean

ATLANTIC CITY

Delaware Bay

Cape May

farms grow the food for its neighbors, New York and Pennsylvania. It makes their products, too. New Jersey is said to make more different kinds of things than any other state.

Surely, New Jersey has more Oranges than Florida: West Orange, South Orange, East Orange, and just plain Orange. In West Orange, we visited a museum dedicated to Thomas Edison. Try to imagine life without lights, records, and movies, and you'll thank Edison for inventing the lightbulb, the phonograph, and the motion picture camera. Invention, he said, was "one percent inspiration and 99 percent perspiration." That means it's hard work, not just waiting around for a lightbulb to go on over your head—ha ha ha.

Thomas Alva Edison

Also "invented" in New Jersey was baseball—the world's first professional baseball game was played in Hoboken. Other famous New Jerseyans include writers Judy Blume and Edward Stratemeyer, who created series of books about Tom Swift, the Hardy Boys, and Nancy Drew. Walt Whitman spent the last 20 years of his life in this state.

And it's true—George Washington slept here. So many Revolutionary War battles were fought in New Jersey that it was known as the Cockpit of the American Revolution. The most famous image is that of General Washington crossing the Delaware River during the Battle of Trenton in 1776.

Now commuters cross bridges over the Delaware, going to work in Philadelphia. Others, the "bridge and tunnel people," take the Lincoln and Holland Tunnels or the George Washington Bridge into New York City. New Jersey has a greater percentage of people living in suburbs than any other state. It's one of the smallest states, but it's the most crowded. Among other people, it has Boy Scouts—New Brunswick is their national headquarters—and soup eaters. We visited the Campbell Museum in Camden, learning all about the history of soup . . . we ate some, too.

FAMOUS NEW JERSEY QUOTATION

"The Garden of Eden was actually located ten miles below Jersey City, just off the New Jersey Turnpike. . . . That is why they call this the Garden State!"
—New Jersey singer and songwriter Bruce Springsteen

The George Washington Bridge

Connecticut

Grandma and I noticed something old-fashioned about Connecticut. All the country towns center around a village green, which is a park. There's always a little white church nearby, a town meeting hall, sometimes a schoolhouse.

We had a fine "old" time at Mystic Seaport, a museum that includes an old whaling village. Some of America's great sailing ships were built here. I rolled hoops and tossed rings, playing games from a century ago. A Children's Museum

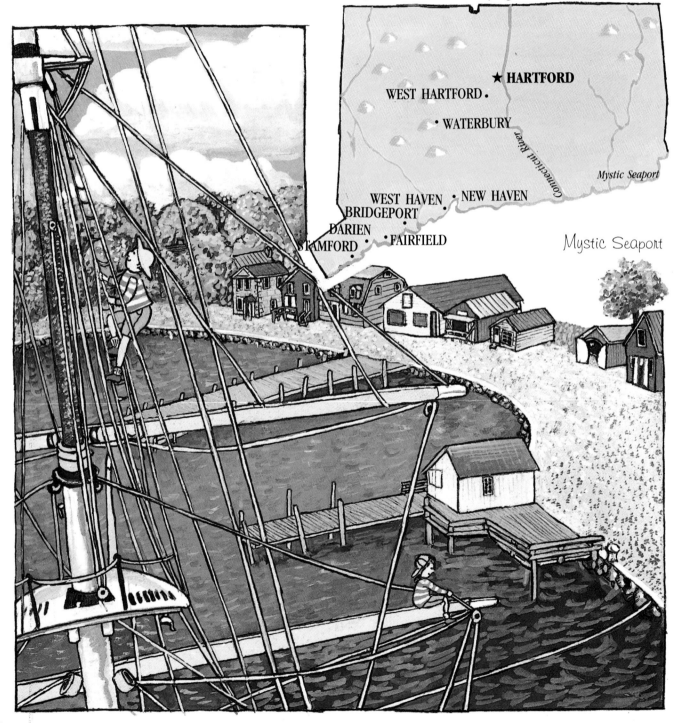

★ **HARTFORD**

WEST HARTFORD •

• WATERBURY

Connecticut River

Mystic Seaport

WEST HAVEN • NEW HAVEN
BRIDGEPORT •
DARIEN
STAMFORD • • FAIRFIELD

Mystic Seaport

CAPITAL: **Hartford**

MOTTO: *Qui Transtulit Sustinet*
(**He Who Transplanted Still Sustains**)

let me imagine what it was like to be a child going to sea. Later, we munched apples (Connecticut's most important fruit) and had fresh apple cider with our Yankee pot roast.

"Yankee Doodle" is the Connecticut state song, and "Yankee ingenuity" was important here. The first American public school was in Connecticut, and this was the first state to elect a woman governor who wasn't related to a man governor—Ella Grasso. Connecticut workers were the first Americans to make bicycles, Silly Putty, Frisbees—and lollipops! Hmm . . . maybe that's why P. T. Barnum from Bridgeport, the great circus man, said, "There's a sucker born every minute." This was the home of Eli Whitney, the inventor of the cotton gin, and Charles Goodyear, who found a way to strengthen rubber in 1839. And who could forget Sylvester Graham, who invented the graham cracker.

Connecticut may be the third-smallest state, but it's one of the richest ones, in per-person income. Many people work in New York City; we saw trains taking thousands of businesspeople away. Businesses like it here, too, especially in Darien, Stamford, and Fairfield. Hartford is the Insurance City, home to 50 insurance companies. Almost all people in Connecticut were born in America; Italian Americans make up one of the state's largest ethnic groups.

Two-thirds of Connecticut is forest—thickets of birch, alder, and goldenrod. There's also the dogwood—which sounds like a tree full of poodles, but is really a pretty tree that flowers in May.

WRITING IN CONNECTICUT

1. The *Children's Magazine,* the first American publication for children, was published here in 1789.

2. Harriet Beecher Stowe, famous for *Uncle Tom's Cabin,* was born in Litchfield and lived for years in Hartford.

3. Her next-door neighbor was Mark Twain, who built and designed a fancy mansion, where he wrote *The Adventures of Tom Sawyer, Adventures of Huckleberry Finn,* and *A Connecticut Yankee in King Arthur's Court,* which made fun of Bridgeport.

4. Also in Hartford, the first cookbook ever written by an American was published: *American Cookery* by Amelia Simmons in 1796.

5. Nearby, in West Hartford, was born Noah Webster—you know, as in Webster's Dictionary? His first book, published in 1783, was *Blue-Backed Speller.*

6. Eleanor Estes was the children's librarian at the New Haven Public Library. In all those great books about the Moffats, she modeled the town of Cranbury after West Haven.

Town

Country

Rhode Island

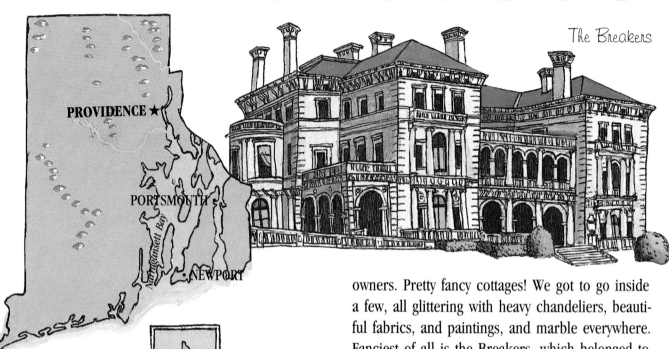

The Breakers

Rhode Island seems like a nice quiet place—half forest, and so small that I'll bet everyone knows everyone else. It may be America's littlest state, but it's great in other ways. It has more than 100 beaches for swimming . . . and the most famous playground of all: Newport, where America's first millionaires had their summer homes. Grandma said that parties in Newport used to be the fantasy life America dreamed about, the way movies are now.

We had our own party, a traditional Yankee clambake. The clams get smothered by seaweed and sizzled on hot rocks on the beach, till they're soft and tasty. Then we took the famous three-mile Cliff Walk, breathing the salty air and listening to the Atlantic Ocean waves pounding. These gorgeous palaces, with their lawns rolling down to the sea, were called "cottages" by their

owners. Pretty fancy cottages! We got to go inside a few, all glittering with heavy chandeliers, beautiful fabrics, and paintings, and marble everywhere. Fanciest of all is the Breakers, which belonged to the Astors, all 72 rooms.

One important Newport person was Clement C. Moore, author of *A Visit from St. Nicholas,* which begins, " 'Twas the night before Christmas." His summer home is now a museum of children's toys.

Rhode Island is spunky. I mean, this state de-

Having our own Yankee clambake!

CAPITAL: **Providence**

MOTTO: **Hope**

Touro Synagogue in Newport, oldest synagogue in the U.S.A.

Newport's Trinity Church; George Washington prayed here

clared itself independent of England two whole months before everyone else: Independence Day here is May 4, not July 4. Rhode Island has the highest percentage of Roman Catholics, and of people with foreign-born parents, especially Irish, Portuguese, and French Canadians. They stay put: Rhode Islanders move less often than people in any other state.

Grandma and I bought lots of costume jewelry as souvenirs. We were in one of the world's largest costume jewelry centers. Then we ate a breakfast of Portuguese sweet bread and special Rhode Island johnnycake. This white cornmeal treat comes from what travelers used to stock up on: journeycakes. That was us . . . off on the next part of our journey.

ODD FACTS ABOUT RHODE ISLAND

1. It's not an island. Instead, it's 36 small islands and one big mainland, almost cut in two by Narragansett Bay.

2. Roger Williams, considered the founder of Rhode Island, and his wife were buried on their farm. Many years later, their graves were dug up when Rhode Islanders wanted to give them a fancier resting place. Here's the odd part: The graves were empty! An apple tree nearby had grown huge, its roots apparently fertilized by Mr. and Mrs. Williams.

3. If you were a baby, your best chances for a long life would be in Rhode Island. This state has the lowest infant death rate.

4. H. P. Lovecraft, who wrote scary stories, used to wander around a Providence cemetery—getting ideas, I guess. You know who used to wander through the same cemetery? *Another* horror writer, Edgar Allan Poe. Maybe he was thinking up ideas, too, for poems and stories like "The Raven" and "The Tell-Tale Heart." Eeeks!

Massachusetts

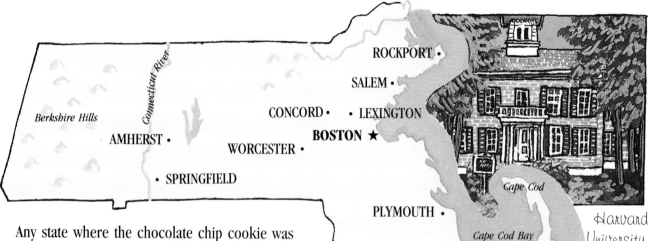

ROCKPORT •
SALEM •
CONCORD • • LEXINGTON
BOSTON ★
WORCESTER •
AMHERST •
• SPRINGFIELD
Berkshire Hills
Connecticut River
PLYMOUTH •
Cape Cod
Cape Cod Bay
• **NEW BEDFORD**
Martha's Vineyard
Nantucket
Atlantic Ocean • **NANTUCKET**

Harvard University, Cambridge, oldest college in the U.S.A.

Any state where the chocolate chip cookie was invented is okay with me. Or a state that gave birth to three presidents named John (Kennedy, Adams, and Quincy Adams). Or a doctor named Seuss (Theodore Geisel).

Grandma loves Massachusetts for its writers. Louisa May Alcott, who wrote *Little Women,* is buried in Sleepy Hollow Cemetery, along with many other writers. Born in Boston were Edgar Allan Poe; Ralph Waldo Emerson; Benjamin Franklin; the poet Sylvia Plath; and Lucretia Hale, who wrote stories Grandma likes called *The Peterkin Papers.* Robert McCloskey's *Make Way for Ducklings* is about a family of mallards in Boston's Public Garden.

Nathaniel Hawthorne was born in Salem and based *The House of the Seven Gables* on a real house there. In the Salem witch trials of 1692,

20 witches were killed; today, 350 people who call themselves witches live there. Amherst is famous because of poet Emily Dickinson, and Herman Melville's *Moby-Dick* was inspired by the whaling ports of New Bedford and Nantucket.

Grandma and I hiked Boston's Freedom Trail. It's a redbrick path that starts at Boston Common, the oldest public park in America. It winds through downtown to places where history was made: Faneuil Hall, the Paul Revere House, Old North Church, the Old Corner Bookstore.

We stopped for real New England chowder—a thick soup of milk, potatoes, and clams, with special crackers called common crackers. For dessert, Grandma had Boston cream pie. I had

<u>Make Way for Ducklings</u> statue, Boston Public Garden

CAPITAL: **Boston**

MOTTO: *Ense Petit Placidam Sub Libertate Quietem*
*(By the Sword We Seek Peace, but Peace Only
Under Liberty)*

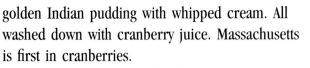

golden Indian pudding with whipped cream. All washed down with cranberry juice. Massachusetts is first in cranberries.

Cape Cod has a funny hook shape, maybe because it's so good for fishing. It's also great for nature walks, swimming, boating, sailboarding,

Cape Cod

and watching the rich and famous. Some of their houses are 350 years old. Many people on the East Coast dream of summering on Cape Cod. If you're cool you say "the Cape." The sounds and smells of the Atlantic Ocean seem the strongest here.

One place we missed was Rockport, home to Motif No. 1. That's a red fishing warehouse said to be the most painted scene in New England. No wonder so many painters (including Winslow Homer) lived here!

**JUST SOME OF THE FAMOUS MOMENTS
IN MASSACHUSETTS**

1. November 11, 1620, when the Pilgrims arrived from England on the *Mayflower*. They dropped anchor at what is now the tip of Cape Cod.

2. The first Thanksgiving, which 50 Pilgrims celebrated at Plymouth with 90 Wampanoags. These American Indians amazed the Pilgrims with bushels of popcorn. Also served were venison, duck, clams, lobster, and plums.

3. The Boston Tea Party in 1773—not really a party, but an American protest against a British tea tax.

4. Paul Revere's famous 1775 ride to warn Americans, "The British are coming." The next day, the American Revolution began in Lexington and Concord, with the shots "heard round the world."

Paul Revere
in front of
Old North Church

Vermont

Over mugs of apple cider, Grandma and I talked about what to do next in Vermont. Grandma wanted to shop for crafts and clothes with the famous "Made in Vermont" label. I wanted to shop for some Ben & Jerry's ice cream. We compromised. We visited a maple sugarhouse to see how maple syrup is made.

Three-quarters of Vermont is forest, and a lot of those trees are sugar maples. American Indians taught Vermonters how to notch the trees and catch the sweet sap in bark buckets. They dropped hot stones into the sap, boiling it down into syrup. It takes the sap from many trees to make one gallon of syrup.

Now Vermont is the largest producer of maple syrup in America, putting it into cream, cakes, taffy, even salad dressings and barbecue sauce. We bought a small bottle of maple syrup to take home and eat with our pancakes.

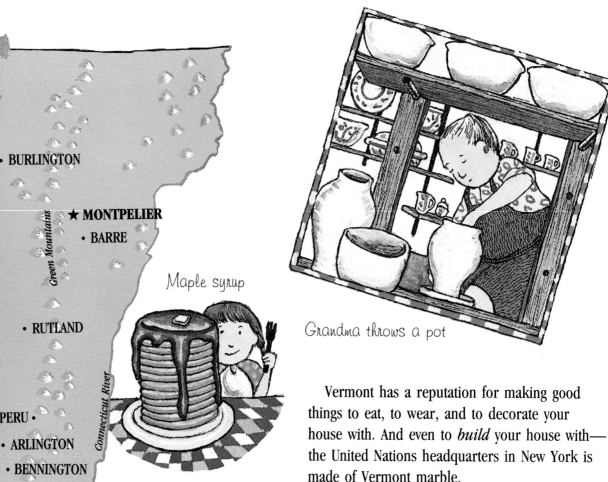

Maple syrup

Grandma throws a pot

Vermont has a reputation for making good things to eat, to wear, and to decorate your house with. And even to *build* your house with— the United Nations headquarters in New York is made of Vermont marble.

Map labels

- BURLINGTON
- ★ MONTPELIER
- BARRE
- RUTLAND
- PERU
- ARLINGTON
- BENNINGTON

Lake Champlain
Green Mountains
Connecticut River

CAPITAL: **Montpelier**

MOTTO: **Freedom and Unity**

A Vermont scene

Vermont has the highest percentage of rural residents of any state, and only Alaska and Wyoming have fewer people. Montpelier is the most sparsely populated state capital in America. On top of the state capitol dome here is a statue of the Roman goddess of farms, Ceres.

This state is so independent that, like Texas, it was its own country for years before joining America. Vermont had its own money, postal service, and relations with foreign countries. Then it became the first state after the original 13 colonies, and went on to become the first state to outlaw slavery and allow all men to vote.

Vermonters know how to play. The longest slide in the world is in Peru—the Bromley Alpine Slide. Tree watchers love Vermont in fall, and skiers love Vermont in winter. The Green Mountains, round and friendly, run through the entire state. It's the only New England state not on the Atlantic Ocean, but the waters of the Connecticut River and Lake Champlain make up for it.

While driving in Vermont, Grandma kept pointing out the famous round barns. To the north, road signs are in English and French, with Quebec just across the border in Canada.

"Vermont is a state of mind," said some of the bumper stickers—I can see what they mean. All over we saw pretty farms and old-fashioned villages that looked as if they belonged on a postcard—things you'd dream about when you were far from Vermont.

PAINTERS LIKE VERMONT

Norman Rockwell lived in Arlington; we saw many of his *Saturday Evening Post* covers and other paintings in an old church here. Local people who modeled for these pictures serve as tour guides. And Bennington has the Grandma Moses Schoolhouse Museum, with paintings by the famous grandmother who started painting at age 78 and never stopped till she was 101.

New Hampshire

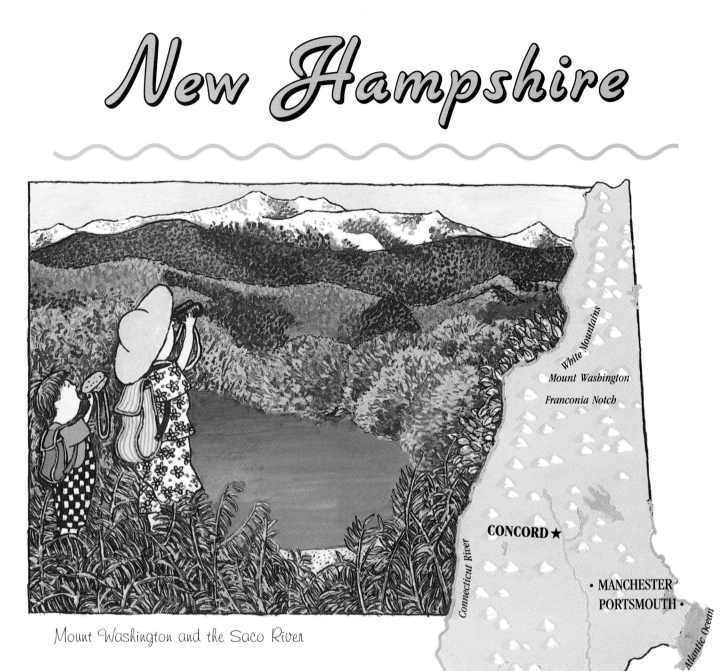

Mount Washington and the Saco River

Not till Columbus Day do the famous trees of New Hampshire really take off, but Grandma and I saw some major hints. I mean *color*—the reds, oranges, purples, and yellows of sugar maples, sumacs, pin cherries, witch hazels, white ashes, and red maples—with some plain green speckled alders just for fun.

We had the best view of all from where we were: Mount Washington in the White Mountains. P. T. Barnum called this "the second greatest show on earth." I could see colorific trees in five New England states; the Atlantic Ocean—New Hampshire has only 13 miles of coastline; and even part of Canada.

These are rugged mountains. They have some of the worst winds and cold in the East. The temperature can drop 50 degrees in minutes, even in summer, and the strongest wind ever recorded was right here—try 231 miles per hour. The perfect symbol for New Hampshire is here: the Old Man of the Mountains, at Franconia Notch. This is a craggy, *huge* stone profile of a man's face, formed by five ledges of the White Mountains.

Grandma said it's mountains like this—and New Hampshire *is* the most mountainous state in New England—that have shaped the people here.

100

CAPITAL: **Concord**

MOTTO: **Live Free or Die**

The Old Man of the Mountains

The New England Yankees and the French Canadians who tamed the New Hampshire wilderness are independent, hardworking, inventive, and fond of a good laugh.

Grandma says nobody can tell a New Hampshirite what to do. This was the first of the original 13 colonies to set up its own government. Famous people from here include Margaret Knight, who invented the brown paper bag; Sara Josepha Hale, famous for writing "Mary Had a Little Lamb"; and Robert Frost, who called the woods "lovely, dark and deep" in his poem "Stopping by Woods on a Snowy Evening." Alan Shepard, the first American astronaut to travel in space, is from here, as was Christa McAuliffe, the Concord teacher chosen to be "citizen in space" on the ill-fated space shuttle *Challenger.*

Politicians care what New Hampshirites think. After the Iowa caucuses, this state has the earliest primary election to select presidential candidates every four years. Rarely does someone become president who loses in New Hampshire.

A New Hampshire mystery: Mystery Hill near Manchester has odd stone slabs and walls. Some people think they date from prehistoric times—evidence of a great civilization that flourished here way before Europeans arrived. Others think an eccentric farmer built them a lot more recently.

And another thing: If this is *New* Hampshire, whatever happened to the *old* one? Grandma said it's where it's supposed to be, in England. Back in 1629, Captain John Mason named this area after the English countryside of Hampshire.

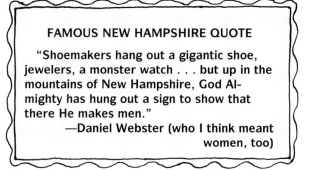

FAMOUS NEW HAMPSHIRE QUOTE

"Shoemakers hang out a gigantic shoe, jewelers, a monster watch . . . but up in the mountains of New Hampshire, God Almighty has hung out a sign to show that there He makes men."
—Daniel Webster (who I think meant women, too)

A village green in Washington

Maine

Know why people in Maine see the sun rise before any other state? Not because they get up so extra early, but because this is the easternmost state in America—and the sun rises in the east. We watched the sunrise from the top of Mount Cadillac, the highest mountain right on America's eastern coastline. We were in Acadia National Park, the only national park where mountains meet the surf.

Maine seems so far away somehow. Only one other state, New Hampshire, touches it. Maine was not an easy place to settle. Grandma said parts of Maine still have no electricity or telephones or even roads. It's a good place to visit if you want to be by yourself and read a good book. I was reading *Charlotte's Web* by E. B. White, written in North Brooklin, and Grandma read *Rebecca of Sunnybrook Farm* by Kate Douglas Wiggin, written in Hollis.

Most visitors go to the coast. The quiet old fishing towns look familiar—probably because of all the seascapes that have been painted in Maine. We talked to one man who was painting a picture of the oldest lighthouse in America, Portland

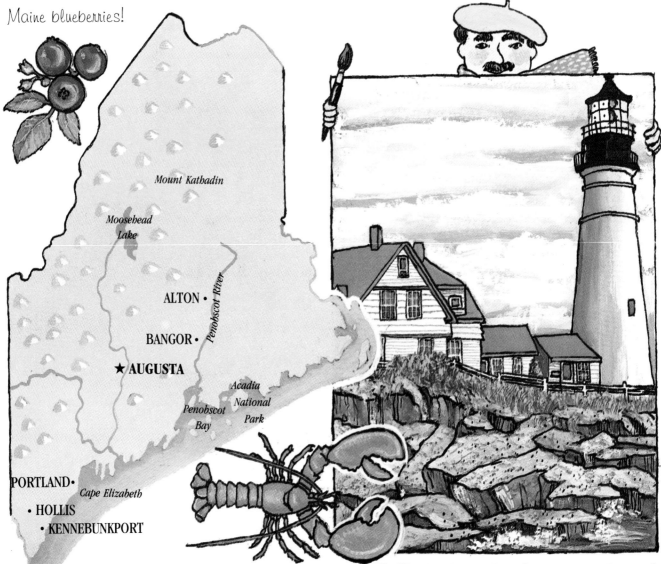

Maine blueberries!

Mount Kathadin

Moosehead Lake

Penobscot River

ALTON •

BANGOR •

★ AUGUSTA

Acadia National Park

Penobscot Bay

PORTLAND•
Cape Elizabeth

• HOLLIS

• KENNEBUNKPORT

The Portland Head Light at Cape Elizabeth

CAPITAL: **Augusta**
MOTTO: *Dirigo* (I Direct)

Head Light at Cape Elizabeth. The painter told us how lighthouses warn ships away from dangerous rocks. This is one of 64 lighthouses in the state. Maine has a *very* rocky shore!

We noticed that right away when we went sailing on the silvery waters of Penobscot Bay. Luckily, it wasn't one of Maine's famous foggy days. We could see the rocky shore clearly enough not to crash into it. Grandma loved the sound of water lapping against the rocks, and the smells of the salty air and pine woods. I loved the seals lined up on a ledge like sunbathers, and the family of ducks floating by. We saw people catching lobsters—Maine is first in lobster—and took care not to get drenched by the salty spray.

We stopped for lunch at an old stagecoach inn. We had hearty chowder, made from quahogs, or mud-loving clams, and pieces of blueberry pie. Most of America's wild blueberries come from Maine. After that we chewed gum: The first chewing gum was made in Maine!

Besides lots of firs for Christmas trees, Maine has wood for jobs both big and small. Gigantic masts for huge ships are made here, as well as more wooden toothpicks than in any other state. Up north, moose watching is the thing to do: Try seven feet tall, with antlers five feet across. Children get out of school early here to help with the harvest, which is mostly potatoes.

Bzzzz . . . the state insect of Maine is the honeybee. And bzzzz . . . my head was buzzing as we turned the little red car around and headed for home, sweet home. *Mainly,* I liked Maine. And mainly, I loved all the United States!

**PLACES DOWN EAST
I WAS SORRY TO MISS**

Kennebunkport, once a shipbuilding port, site of former President George Bush's summer home. I could have eaten his favorite meal: baked stuffed lobster and peanut butter ice cream pie. And Alton, where the Red Paint American Indians of 3000 to 5000 B.C. had a summer settlement. The first vacationers in Maine!

Enjoying the Maine coast

Extra Credit: A Note for My Geography Teacher

Well! Grandma and I going on the road to discover the United States was the wildest summer of my life so far. I learned that the United States is not all just like New York City, or anywhere else. We might all watch the same TV shows, eat at the same fast-food places, or shop at malls with the same stores in them, but each state has lots that no other state does. Every one of the 50 states is totally special, as well as that most unusual place, the District of Columbia.

And, dear geography teacher, I learned that travel really is the best teacher. Besides Grandma. Ooops, and besides you. Geography helped me to understand the United States better than I did before. It taught me why the United States is the way it is—the influence of American Indians, the accomplishments of newer arrivals, the wealth of this land in all its sights, sounds, smells, and—my personal favorite—foods. I found out that geography is a way of learning about pretty much EVERYTHING, from people both famous and ordinary, to history and environment, to sports, science, literature, and all the arts. This trip made me want to travel more—like to Puerto Rico and United States territories like the Virgin Islands—and even to other countries in Europe . . . Asia . . . Africa . . . South America . . . everywhere.

I even learned how to read a map. Oh, and I found out that geography leads to just an amazing amount of fun! Things that will make you say, "Wish you were here!" to everyone you know. Your favorite student,

Emily

How to Get More Information

There is so MUCH I haven't told you about each of the 50 states. Here are places to write to for more information if (lucky you) you're planning to visit any of the states for yourself.

ALABAMA
Alabama Bureau of Tourism
  and Travel
401 Adams Street
Montgomery, AL 36103-4309
  (phone: 1-800-ALABAMA)

ALASKA
Alaska Division of Tourism
P.O. Box 110801
Juneau, AK 99811-0801
  (phone: 907-465-2012,
  a toll call; fax 907-465-2287)

ARIZONA
Arizona Office of Tourism
2702 N. Third St., Suite 4015
Phoenix, AZ 85004
  (phone: 1-800-842-8257)

ARKANSAS
Arkansas Department of Parks
  and Tourism
One Capitol Mall
Little Rock, AR 72201
  (phone: 1-800-NATURAL)

CALIFORNIA
California Division of Tourism
801 K Street, #1600
Sacramento, CA 95812
  (phone: 1-800-862-2543)

COLORADO
Colorado Tourism and Travel
  Administration
P.O. Box 3524
Englewood, CO 80155
  (phone: 1-800-433-2656)

CONNECTICUT
Department of Economic
  Development
865 Brook Street
Rocky Hill, CT 06067-3405
  (phone: 1-800-CT-BOUND)

DELAWARE
Delaware Tourism Office
99 Kings Highway
Box 1401
Dover, DE 19903
  (phone: 1-800-441-8846)

DISTRICT OF COLUMBIA
Washington, D.C., Convention
  and Visitors Association
1212 New York Avenue, NW
Washington, D.C. 20005
  (phone: 202-789-7000,
  a toll call)

FLORIDA
Florida Department of Commerce,
  Division of Tourism
126 West Van Buren Street
Tallahassee, FL 32399-2000
  (phone: 904-487-1462,
  a toll call)

GEORGIA
The Georgia Hospitality and Travel
  Association
P.O. Box 1776
Atlanta, GA 30301-1776
  (phone: 1-800-VISIT-GA)

HAWAII
Hawaii Visitors Bureau
2270 Kalakaua Avenue, 8th Floor
Honolulu, HI 96815
  (phone: 808-923-1811,
  a toll call)

IDAHO
Idaho Travel Council
Administrative Office
Idaho Department of Commerce
700 West State Street
P.O. Box 83720
Boise, ID 83720-0093
  (phone: 1-800-635-7820)

ILLINOIS
Illinois Department of Commerce
Historical Watertower
806 N. Michigan Avenue
Chicago, IL 60604
  (phone: 1-800-226-6632)

INDIANA
Indiana Department of Commerce
Tourism Development Division
One Hoosier Dome, #100
Indianapolis, IN 46225
  (phone: 1-800-289-ONIN)

IOWA
Bureau of Tourism and Visitors
Department of Economic
  Development
200 E. Grand Avenue
Des Moines, IA 50309
  (phone: 1-800-345-IOWA)

KANSAS
Kansas Department of Commerce
  and Housing
Division of Kansas Tourism
700 S.W. Harrison Street,
  Suite 1300
Topeka, KS 66603
  (phone: 1-800-252-6727)

KENTUCKY
Kentucky Department of Travel
  Development
Capital Plaza Tower
500 Mero Street
Frankfort, KY 40601
  (phone: 1-800-225-TRIP)

LOUISIANA
Department of Culture, Recreation,
  and Tourism
1051 N. 3rd Street
Capital Annex Building
Baton Rouge, LA 70802
  (phone: 1-800-33-GUMBO)

MAINE
The Maine Publicity Bureau, Inc.
P.O. Box 2300
Hallowell, ME 04347
  (phone: 1-800-533-9595)

MARYLAND
Office of Tourism Development
217 East Redwood Street,
  9th Floor
Baltimore, MD 21233
  (phone: 1-800-543-1036)

MASSACHUSETTS
Massachusetts Division of Tourism
100 Cambridge Street, 13th Floor
Boston, MA 02202
  (phone: 1-800-447-MASS)

MICHIGAN
Michigan Travel Bureau
P.O. Box 30226
Lansing, MI 48909
  (phone: 1-800-5432-YES)

MINNESOTA
Minnesota Office of Tourism
100 Metro Square
121 E. 7th Place
St. Paul, MN 55101
  (phone: 1-800-657-3700)

MISSISSIPPI
Mississippi Department of Tourism
P.O. Box 1705
Ocean Springs, MS 39566
  (phone: 1-800-927-6378)

MISSOURI
Missouri Division of Tourism
Truman State Office Building
P.O. Box 1055
Jefferson City, MO 65102
  (phone: 314-751-4133,
  a toll call)

MONTANA
Travel 'Montana
1424 9th Avenue
Helena, MT 59620
  (phone: 1-800-541-1447)

NEBRASKA
Nebraska Department of Economic
  Development
Division of Travel and Tourism
P.O. Box 94666
Lincoln, NE 68509
  (phone: 1-800-228-4307)

NEVADA
Nevada Commission on Tourism
Capitol Complex
Carson City, NV 89710
  (phone: 1-800-NEVADA-8)

NEW HAMPSHIRE
New Hampshire Office of Travel
  and Tourism Development
P.O. Box 1856
Concord, NH 03302-1856
  (phone: 1-800-386-4664)

NEW JERSEY
New Jersey Department
  of Commerce
Division of Travel and Tourism
CN 826
20 West State Street
Trenton, NJ 08625
  (phone: 1-800-JERSEY-7)

NEW MEXICO
New Mexico Department
  of Tourism
491 Old Sante Fe Trail
Santa Fe, NM 87503
  (phone: 1-800-545-2040)

NEW YORK
New York State Hospitality and
  Tourism Association
11 N. Pearl Street, 11th Floor
Albany, NY 12207
  (phone: 518-465-2300,
  a toll call)

NORTH CAROLINA
North Carolina Division of Travel
  and Tourism
430 North Salisbury Street
Raleigh, NC 27603
  (phone: 1-800-VISIT-NC)

NORTH DAKOTA
North Dakota Tourism
604 East Boulevard
Bismarck, ND 58505
  (phone: 1-800-437-2077)

OHIO
Division of Travel and Tourism
77 High Street
Columbus, OH 43215
  (phone: 1-800-BUCKEYE)

OKLAHOMA
Oklahoma Tourism
P.O. Box 60789
Oklahoma City, OK 73146-9910
  (phone: 1-800-652-6552)

OREGON
Oregon Tourism Commission
775 Summer Street NE
Salem, OR 97310
  (phone: 1-800-547-7842)

PENNSYLVANIA
Pennsylvania Department of
  Commerce
Bureau of Travel Marketing
Room 453, Forum Building
Harrisburg, PA 17120
  (phone: 1-800-VISIT-PA)

RHODE ISLAND
Rhode Island Tourism Division
1 West Exchange Street
Providence, RI 02903
  (phone: 1-800-556-2484)

SOUTH CAROLINA
South Carolina Division of Tourism
P.O. Box 71
Columbia, SC 29202
  (phone: 803-734-0235,
  a toll call)

SOUTH DAKOTA
South Dakota Tourism
711 E. Wells Avenue
Pierre, SD, 57501
  (phone: 1-800-S-DAKOTA)

TENNESSEE
Tennessee Department of Tourism
Rachel Jackson Building, 5th Floor
320 6th Avenue North
Nashville, TN 37204-3170
    (phone: 615-741-2158,
    a toll call)

TEXAS
State Department of Highways
    and Public Transportation
Travel and Tourism Division
P.O. Box 5064
Austin, TX 78763-5064
    (phone: 1-800-8888-TEX)

UTAH
Utah Travel Council
Council Hall
Capitol Hill
Salt Lake City, UT 84114
    (phone: 801-538-1030,
    a toll call)

VERMONT
Vermont Chamber of Commerce
P.O. Box 37
Montpelier, VT 05601-0037
    (phone: 802-223-3443,
    a toll call)

VIRGINIA
Division of Tourism
1021 E. Cary Street, 14th Floor
Richmond, VA 23219
    (phone: 1-800-VISIT-VA)

WASHINGTON
Travel Development Division
101 General Administration
    Building AX-13
P.O. Box 42500
Olympia, WA 98504
    (phone: 1-800-544-1800)

WEST VIRGINIA
Travel West Virginia
State Capitol Complex
Charleston, WV 25305
    (phone: 1-800-CALL-WVA)

WISCONSIN
Wisconsin Tourism Development
123 W. Washington Avenue
P.O. Box 7976
Madison, WI 53707
    (phone: 1-800-432-TRIP)

WYOMING
Wyoming Travel Commission
I-25 at College Drive
Cheyenne, WY 82002
    (phone: 1-800-225-5996)

State Facts

STATE	BIRD	FLOWER	TREE	NICKNAMES
ALABAMA	yellowhammer	camellia	southern pine	Heart of Dixie, Cotton State, Yellowhammer State, Camellia State
ALASKA	Alaska willow ptarmigan	forget-me-not	sitka spruce	The Last Frontier
ARIZONA	cactus wren	saguaro (giant cactus) blossom	paloverde	Grand Canyon State
ARKANSAS	mockingbird	apple blossom	pine	Land of Opportunity, Wonder State
CALIFORNIA	California valley quail	golden poppy	California redwood	Golden State
COLORADO	lark bunting	Rocky Mountain columbine	Colorado blue spruce	Centennial State
CONNECTICUT	American robin	mountain laurel	white oak	Constitution State, Nutmeg State
DELAWARE	blue hen chicken	peach blossom	American holly	First State, Diamond State
FLORIDA	mockingbird	orange blossom	Sabal palmetto palm	Sunshine State, Peninsula State, Everglade State
GEORGIA	brown thrasher	Cherokee rose	live oak	Empire State of the South, Peach State
HAWAII	Hawaiian goose	hibiscus	kukui (candlenut) tree	Aloha State
IDAHO	mountain bluebird	syringa	western white pine	Gem State
ILLINOIS	cardinal	native violet	white oak	Prairie State, Inland Empire
INDIANA	cardinal	peony	tulip poplar	Hoosier State
IOWA	eastern goldfinch	wild rose	oak	Hawkeye State

STATE	BIRD	FLOWER	TREE	NICKNAMES
KANSAS	western meadowlark	sunflower	cottonwood	Sunflower State
KENTUCKY	cardinal	goldenrod	Kentucky coffee tree	Bluegrass State
LOUISIANA	eastern brown pelican	magnolia blossom	bald cypress	Pelican State, Creole State, Sugar State
MAINE	chickadee	white pine cone and tassel	eastern white pine	Pine Tree State, Vacationland
MARYLAND	Baltimore oriole	black-eyed Susan	white oak	Old Line State
MASSACHUSETTS	chickadee	mayflower	American elm	Bay State
MICHIGAN	robin	apple blossom	white pine	Wolverine State
MINNESOTA	common loon	lady's slipper	red pine	North Star State, Gopher State
MISSISSIPPI	mockingbird	magnolia	magnolia	Magnolia State
MISSOURI	bluebird	hawthorn	dogwood	Show Me State
MONTANA	western meadowlark	bitterroot	ponderosa pine	Treasure State, Big Sky Country
NEBRASKA	western meadowlark	goldenrod	cottonwood	Cornhusker State
NEVADA	mountain bluebird	sagebrush	single-leaf piñon	Silver State
NEW HAMPSHIRE	purple finch	purple lilac	white birch	Granite State
NEW JERSEY	eastern goldfinch	purple violet	red oak	Garden State
NEW MEXICO	roadrunner	yucca	piñon	Land of Enchantment
NEW YORK	bluebird	rose	sugar maple	Empire State

STATE	BIRD	FLOWER	TREE	NICKNAMES
NORTH CAROLINA	cardinal	dogwood	pine	Tar Heel State
NORTH DAKOTA	western meadowlark	wild prairie rose	American elm	Flickertail State, Sioux State, Peace Garden State
OHIO	cardinal	scarlet carnation	buckeye	Buckeye State
OKLAHOMA	scissor-tailed flycatcher	mistletoe	redbud	Sooner State
OREGON	western meadowlark	Oregon grape	Douglas fir	Beaver State
PENNSYLVANIA	ruffed grouse	mountain laurel	eastern hemlock	Keystone State
RHODE ISLAND	Rhode Island red	violet	red maple	Little Rhody, Ocean State
SOUTH CAROLINA	Carolina wren	Carolina jessamine	palmetto	Palmetto State
SOUTH DAKOTA	ring-necked pheasant	pasque flower	Black Hills spruce	Coyote State, Sunshine State, Land of Infinite Variety
TENNESSEE	mockingbird	iris	tulip poplar	Big Bend State, Volunteer State
TEXAS	mockingbird	bluebonnet	pecan	Lone Star State
UTAH	seagull	sego lily	blue spruce	Beehive State
VERMONT	hermit thrush	red clover	sugar maple	Green Mountain State
VIRGINIA	cardinal	American dogwood	American dogwood	The Old Dominion
WASHINGTON	willow goldfinch	western rhododendron	western hemlock	Evergreen State
WEST VIRGINIA	cardinal	rhododendron	sugar maple	Mountain State
WISCONSIN	robin	wood violet	sugar maple	Badger State
WYOMING	meadowlark	Indian paintbrush	cottonwood	Equality State, Cowboy State

When Each State Became a State

STATE	YEAR OF STATEHOOD	ORDER IN WHICH IT JOINED THE UNITED STATES	HOW THE STATE PROBABLY GOT ITS NAME
ALABAMA	1819	22nd	from Choctaw Indian *alba ayamule*, "I open the thicket"
ALASKA	1959	49th	from the Inuit *alakshak* or *alayeska*—"great land"
ARIZONA	1912	48th	from the Papago Indian *arizonac*—"small springs"
ARKANSAS	1836	25th	Sioux Indian for "land of the south wind people"
CALIFORNIA	1850	31st	from a popular 16th-century Spanish novel featuring Queen Calafia
COLORADO	1876	38th	from the Spanish *rio colorado*—"reddish river"
CONNECTICUT	1788	5th	from the Mohican Indian *quinnitukqut*—"at the long tidal river"
DELAWARE	1787	1st	after Thomas West, Baron De La Warr, an English governor of Virginia
FLORIDA	1845	27th	Spanish for land of the flowers, also "flowery Easter"
GEORGIA	1788	4th	named for King George II of England
HAWAII	1959	50th	Polynesian *hawaiki*—"homeland"
IDAHO	1890	43rd	Shoshone Indian for "light on the mountains"
ILLINOIS	1818	21st	via French from Algonquian Indian *iliniwek*—"superior men, warriors"
INDIANA	1816	19th	"land of the Indians"

STATE	YEAR OF STATEHOOD	ORDER IN WHICH IT JOINED THE UNITED STATES	HOW THE STATE PROBABLY GOT ITS NAME
IOWA	1846	29th	from Dakota Indian *ayuhwa*—"the sleepy ones"
KANSAS	1861	34th	via French *Kansas* and Spanish *Escansque* from Sioux Indian for "land of the south wind people"
KENTUCKY	1792	15th	from Iroquois Indian *kentake*—"meadowland"
LOUISIANA	1812	18th	named for King Louis XIV of France
MAINE	1820	23rd	named for a French province
MARYLAND	1788	7th	"Marieland," named for Henrietta Marie of French and English royal families
MASSACHUSETTS	1788	6th	from Algonquian Indian for "place of the big hill"
MICHIGAN	1837	26th	from Chippewa Indian *mica gama*, or "big water"
MINNESOTA	1858	32nd	from Sioux Indian for "sky blue water"
MISSISSIPPI	1817	20th	from Chippewa Indian *mici sibi*, or "big river"
MISSOURI	1821	24th	from Algonquian Indian for "muddy water"
MONTANA	1889	41st	Spanish for "mountainous"
NEBRASKA	1867	37th	from Omaha Indian *nibthaska*, or "river in the flatness," meaning the Platte River
NEVADA	1864	36th	Spanish for "snowy"
NEW HAMPSHIRE	1788	9th	Named for Hampshire County, England, by Captain John Mason

STATE	YEAR OF STATEHOOD	ORDER IN WHICH IT JOINED THE UNITED STATES	HOW THE STATE PROBABLY GOT ITS NAME
NEW JERSEY	1787	3rd	Named for the Isle of Jersey off the coast of England
NEW MEXICO	1912	47th	named by Spanish explorers from Mexico
NEW YORK	1788	11th	named after the Duke of York, to whom the land was given by his brother, King Charles II of England
NORTH CAROLINA	1789	12th	Named for King Charles I of England (Latinized as Carolina)
NORTH DAKOTA	1889	39th	Sioux Indians called themselves Dakota, which means "friends"
OHIO	1803	17th	from Iroquois Indian *Oheo*, for "beautiful, beautiful water," meaning the Ohio River
OKLAHOMA	1907	46th	Choctaw Indian for "the Red People"
OREGON	1850	33rd	from Algonquian Indian *Wauregan*, for "beautiful water," meaning the Colorado River
PENNSYLVANIA	1787	2nd	Named for William Penn, and the Latin *sylva*, or "wood"
RHODE ISLAND	1790	13th	Dutch for "red clay island"
SOUTH CAROLINA	1788	8th	Named for King Charles I of England (Latinized as Carolina)
SOUTH DAKOTA	1889	40th	Sioux Indians called themselves Dakota, meaning "friends"
TENNESSEE	1796	16th	from Tanasi, a Cherokee village

STATE	YEAR OF STATEHOOD	ORDER IN WHICH IT JOINED THE UNITED STATES	HOW THE STATE PROBABLY GOT ITS NAME
TEXAS	1845	28th	from *tejas* (Spanish) and *texia* (the local American Indian word for "friend")
UTAH	1896	45th	Named for the Ute Indians
VERMONT	1791	14th	French *vert mont,* or "green mountain"
VIRGINIA	1788	10th	Named for Elizabeth I of England, the "Virgin Queen"
WASHINGTON	1889	42nd	Named for George Washington
WEST VIRGINIA	1863	35th	Named for Elizabeth I of England, the "Virgin Queen"
WISCONSIN	1848	30th	Algonquian Indian for "grassy place" or "place of the beaver"
WYOMING	1890	44th	from Algonquian Indian *macheweaming,* "at the big flats"

Suggestions for Further Reading

Aylesworth, Thomas. *The Kids' World Almanac of the United States*. New York: Pharos Books, 1990.

Black, Sonia. *Across the U.S.A. Game*. New York: Scholastic, 1989.

Bloch, S. *Fabulous Facts About Fifty States*. New York: Scholastic, 1991.

Brownstone, David. *Natural Wonders of America*. New York: Atheneum, 1989.

Caney, Steven. *Kids' America*. New York: Workman, 1978.

Carpenter, Allan. *Far-flung America*. Chicago: Childrens Press, 1979.

———. The New Enchantment of America State Books series. A book for each state. Chicago: Childrens Press, 1978–79.

Cohn, Amy, comp. *From Sea to Shining Sea: A Treasury of American Folklore and Folk Songs*. New York: Scholastic, 1993.

Elwood, Ann, and Carol Madigan. *The Macmillan Book of Fascinating Facts: An Almanac for Kids*. A kid's trip guide to the United States. New York: Macmillan, 1989.

The Gulliver Travels series: *A Kid's Guide to Florida; A Kid's Guide to Southern California; A Kid's Guide to Washington, D.C.; A Kid's Guide to New York City*. San Diego: Harcourt Brace Jovanovich, 1988, 1989.

The Kidding Around series: *A Young Person's Guide* to numerous American cities. Santa Fe: John Muir Publications, 1989–92.

Krull, Kathleen. *Gonna Sing My Head Off: American Folk Songs for Children*. New York: Knopf, 1992.

Perl, Lila. *It Happened in America: True Stories from the Fifty States*. New York: Holt, 1992.

Ronan, Margaret. *All about Our Fifty States*. New York: Random House, 1978.

Ross, Wilma. *Fabulous Facts about the Fifty States*. New York: Scholastic, 1981.

The Young People's Atlas of the United States. New York: Kingfisher, 1992.

Index